Police Training to Promote the Rule of Law and Protect the Population

Committee on Evidence to Advance Reform in the
Global Security and Justice Sectors

Committee on Law and Justice

Division of Behavioral and Social Sciences and Education

A Consensus Study Report of

The National Academies of
SCIENCES • ENGINEERING • MEDICINE

THE NATIONAL ACADEMIES PRESS
Washington, DC
www.nap.edu

THE NATIONAL ACADEMIES PRESS   500 Fifth Street, NW   Washington, DC 20001

This activity was supported by contracts between the National Academy of Sciences and the Bureau of International Narcotics and Law Enforcement Affairs of the U.S. Department of State, Award No. SINLEC20CA3213. Any opinions, findings, conclusions, or recommendations expressed in this publication do not necessarily reflect the views of any organization or agency that provided support for the project.

International Standard Book Number-13: 978-0-309-27751-8
International Standard Book Number-10: 0-309-27751-5
Digital Object Identifier: https://doi.org/10.17226/26467

Additional copies of this publication are available from the National Academies Press, 500 Fifth Street, NW, Keck 360, Washington, DC 20001; (800) 624-6242 or (202) 334-3313; http://www.nap.edu.

Copyright 2022 by the National Academy of Sciences. All rights reserved.

Printed in the United States of America

Suggested citation: National Academies of Sciences, Engineering, and Medicine. 2022. *Police Training to Promote the Rule of Law and Protect the Population.* Washington, DC: The National Academies Press. https://doi.org/10.17226/26467.

The National Academies of
SCIENCES · ENGINEERING · MEDICINE

The **National Academy of Sciences** was established in 1863 by an Act of Congress, signed by President Lincoln, as a private, nongovernmental institution to advise the nation on issues related to science and technology. Members are elected by their peers for outstanding contributions to research. Dr. Marcia McNutt is president.

The **National Academy of Engineering** was established in 1964 under the charter of the National Academy of Sciences to bring the practices of engineering to advising the nation. Members are elected by their peers for extraordinary contributions to engineering. Dr. John L. Anderson is president.

The **National Academy of Medicine** (formerly the Institute of Medicine) was established in 1970 under the charter of the National Academy of Sciences to advise the nation on medical and health issues. Members are elected by their peers for distinguished contributions to medicine and health. Dr. Victor J. Dzau is president.

The three Academies work together as the **National Academies of Sciences, Engineering, and Medicine** to provide independent, objective analysis and advice to the nation and conduct other activities to solve complex problems and inform public policy decisions. The National Academies also encourage education and research, recognize outstanding contributions to knowledge, and increase public understanding in matters of science, engineering, and medicine.

Learn more about the National Academies of Sciences, Engineering, and Medicine at **www.nationalacademies.org**.

The National Academies of
SCIENCES • ENGINEERING • MEDICINE

Consensus Study Reports published by the National Academies of Sciences, Engineering, and Medicine document the evidence-based consensus on the study's statement of task by an authoring committee of experts. Reports typically include findings, conclusions, and recommendations based on information gathered by the committee and the committee's deliberations. Each report has been subjected to a rigorous and independent peer-review process and it represents the position of the National Academies on the statement of task.

Proceedings published by the National Academies of Sciences, Engineering, and Medicine chronicle the presentations and discussions at a workshop, symposium, or other event convened by the National Academies. The statements and opinions contained in proceedings are those of the participants and are not endorsed by other participants, the planning committee, or the National Academies.

For information about other products and activities of the National Academies, please visit www.nationalacademies.org/about/whatwedo.

COMMITTEE ON EVIDENCE TO ADVANCE REFORM IN THE GLOBAL SECURITY AND JUSTICE SECTORS

LAWRENCE W. SHERMAN (*Chair*), University of Cambridge Institute of Criminology
BEATRIZ ABIZANDA, Inter-American Development Bank
YANILDA MARÍA GONZÁLEZ, Kennedy School of Government, Harvard University
GUY GROSSMAN, University of Pennsylvania
JOHN L. HAGAN, Northwestern University
KAREN HALL, Rule of Law Collaborative, University of South Carolina
CYNTHIA LUM, George Mason University
EMILY OWENS, University of California, Irvine
JUSTICE TANKEBE, University of Cambridge Institute of Criminology

JULIE ANNE SCHUCK, *Study Director*
JESSALYN BROGAN WALKER, *Study Director (through June 2021)*
SARAH PERUMATTAM, *Senior Program Assistant (through October 2021)*
SUNIA YOUNG, *Senior Program Assistant (from October 2021)*
ABIGAIL ALLEN, *Associate Program Officer (from November 2021)*
EMILY P. BACKES, *Associate Director, Committee on Law and Justice*
MEGAN SNAIR, *Technical Writer*

COMMITTEE ON LAW AND JUSTICE

ROBERT D. CRUTCHFIELD (*Chair*), University of Washington (*retired*)
SALLY S. SIMPSON (*Vice Chair*), University of Maryland
ROD K. BRUNSON, University of Maryland
SHAWN D. BUSHWAY, University at Albany
PREETI CHAUHAN, John Jay College of Criminal Justice
KIMBERLÉ W. CRENSHAW, University of California, Los Angeles
MARK S. JOHNSON, Howard University
CYNTHIA LUM, George Mason University
JOHN M. MACDONALD, University of Pennsylvania
KAREN J. MATHIS, American Bar Association (*retired*), University of Denver
THEODORE A. MCKEE, United States Court of Appeals for the Third Circuit
SAMUEL L. MYERS, JR., University of Minnesota
EMILY OWENS, University of California, Irvine
CYNTHIA RUDIN, Duke University
WILLIAM J. SABOL, Georgia State University
LINDA A. TEPLIN, Northwestern University Medical School

NATACHA BLAIN, *Director*
EMILY P. BACKES, *Associate Director*

Acknowledgments

This report would not have been possible without the contributions of many people. First, we thank the sponsor of this study, the U.S. Department of State, Bureau of International Narcotics and Law Enforcement Affairs, for requesting and supporting this endeavor. We have admired the sponsor's dedication to an evidence-led approach to further its programming.

Special thanks go to the members of the study committee, who dedicated extensive time, thought, and energy to this report. In addition to its own research and deliberations, the committee received input from several outside sources, whose willingness to share their perspectives and experience was essential to the committee's work. We thank Eric Beinhart (U.S. Department of Justice, International Criminal Investigative Training Assistance Program), Rodrigo Canales (Yale School of Management), Hernán Flom (Trinity College), Grace Long (Nigeria Police Force), Tom Parker (United Nations Office on Drugs and Crime), Jerry Ratcliffe (Temple University), and Scott Wolfe (Michigan State University). The committee also gathered information through two commissioned papers. We thank Lorraine Mazerolle (University of Queensland, Australia) and Tamara D. Herold (University of Nevada, Las Vegas) for their papers and for contributing both to the discussion at the committee's information gathering workshop and to findings in the report.

The committee also wishes to extend its gratitude to the staff of the National Academies of Sciences, Engineering, and Medicine, in particular to Jessalyn Brogan Walker who, as the study director through June 2021, identified and prepared commissioned paper authors and invited speakers for the committee's workshop and began initial report preparations.

Thanks are also due to Julie Schuck who stepped into the study director role mid-project and provided substantive contributions in the conception, writing, and editing of the report. Emily Backes provided substantive writing and editing contributions and oversight and direction for the project. Sarah Perumattam provided key administrative and logistical support and made sure the committee process ran efficiently and smoothly. Sunia Young and Abigail Allen joined the staff while this report was underway and contributed to seeing it finalized while providing administrative support and background research for the activities in the committee's remaining series of workshops and reports. From the Division of Behavioral and Social Sciences and Education, we thank Kirsten Sampson-Snyder, who shepherded the report through the review process, and Douglas Sprunger and Dara Shefska, who assisted with the report's communication and dissemination. We also thank technical writer Megan Snair for quickly summarizing the presentations and discussions from the committee's workshop and editor Marc DeFrancis for their skillful writing and editing of the report manuscript.

This Consensus Study Report was reviewed in draft form by individuals chosen for their diverse perspectives and technical expertise. The purpose of this independent review is to provide candid and critical comments that will assist the National Academies of Sciences, Engineering, and Medicine in making each published report as sound as possible and to ensure that it meets the institutional standards for quality, objectivity, evidence, and responsiveness to the study charge. The review comments and draft manuscript remain confidential to protect the integrity of the deliberative process.

We thank the following individuals for their review of this report: Margaret E. Beier, Psychological Sciences, Rice University; Andrew Faull, Justice and Violence Prevention Programme, Institute for Security Studies; Andrea Fischbach, Department for Social, Work, and Organizational Psychology, German Police University; Matthew J. Hickman, Department of Criminal Justice, Criminology & Forensics, Seattle University; George R. Milner, Department of Anthropology, Pennsylvania State University; Peggy M. Schaefer, National Certification Program, International Association of Directors of Law Enforcement Standards and Training; Clifford Shearing, Department of Public Law, University of Cape Town, Griffith Institute of Criminology and School of Criminology and Criminal Justice, Griffith University, and School of Criminology, University of Montreal; and Michael R. Smith, Department of Criminology & Criminal Justice, The University of Texas at San Antonio.

Although the reviewers listed above provided many constructive comments and suggestions, they were not asked to endorse the conclusions or recommendations of this report nor did they see the final draft before its release. The review of this report was overseen by Alex R. Piquero,

Department of Sociology and Criminology, University of Miami, and Philip J. Cook, Sanford School of Public Policy, Duke University. They were responsible for making certain that an independent examination of this report was carried out in accordance with the standards of the National Academies and that all review comments were carefully considered. Responsibility for the final content rests entirely with the authoring committee and the National Academies.

Contents

SUMMARY	1
1 INTRODUCTION	11
The Committee's Charge, 12	
Evidence-based Policing: Five Principles for Training, 17	
Organization of the Report, 20	
2 REFORM-BASED TRAINING	21
Training-based Reform, 21	
Reform-based Training, 22	
Politics of Police Reform, 23	
Conclusion, 24	
3 KNOWLEDGE AND SKILLS FOR POLICING	27
Supervisory Skills, 29	
Knowledge from Criminology, 30	
Critical Policing Skills, 40	
Conclusion, 46	
4 TRAINING METHODS AND DELIVERY	49
Settings for Police Training, 50	
Problem-solving Techniques, 51	
Instructors, 55	
Training Design, 57	

Evaluations of Training Methods, 60
Conclusion, 64

5 COMMITTEE CONCLUSIONS 65

REFERENCES 73

Appendix Biographical Sketches of Committee Members and Staff 85

Summary

Training police in the knowledge and skills necessary to support the rule of law and protect their publics is a substantial component of the activities of the U.S. Department of State, Bureau of International Narcotics and Law Enforcement Affairs (INL), cognate agencies in other countries, and international organizations that provide foreign assistance. As it designs and delivers training in partner countries, INL depends on the best evidence about both content and methods of training to develop and sustain competent and legitimate criminal justice systems.

However, there are several challenges facing organizations like the INL that support police training in other countries, particularly in the Global South. Significant challenges arise with the wide range of cultural, institutional, political, and social contexts within the countries supported by INL. For example, some countries receiving donor funding may have authoritarian regimes with weak or no commitment to a rule of law (ROL), let alone a priority on protecting the public. In many such places, the police mission is highly focused on protecting the regime in power, by any means necessary, including what may be considered abuses of human rights. In other places, there are modest or even strong signs of movement toward a ROL, and toward greater emphasis on protecting the public. Yet, even these latter countries face myriad institutional obstacles in implementing sought-after reforms. (Institutional obstacles to reform are even present in countries, like the United States, with stronger democratic institutions.)

Another challenge is that foreign assistance donors often have to leverage programs and capacity in their own countries to provide training in partner countries, and there are many examples of training in the Global

North, including the United States, that do not rely on the best scientific evidence of policing practices and training design. Studies have shown disconnects between the reported goals of training, notably that of protecting the population, and actual behaviors by police officers. These realities present a diversity of challenges and opportunities for foreign assistance donors and police training.

As part of its efforts to strengthen policing in the countries it supports, INL asked the Committee on Law and Justice of the National Academies of Sciences, Engineering, and Medicine to convene an ad hoc committee to gather scientific evidence and assess research needs for effective policing in the context of the challenges above. The task of this committee is to review, assess, and reach a consensus on existing evidence on policing institutions, police practices and capacities, and police legitimacy in the international context. The committee was assembled with expertise in criminology, economics, international and organized crime, law, policing, and political science. Its members bring knowledge and experience from a portfolio of work that spans four continents (see Appendix).

The committee was charged to produce a series of five reports addressing questions of interest to INL and the State Department. This second report in the series responds to the following questions: **What are the core knowledge and skills needed for police to promote the ROL and protect the population? What is known about mechanisms (e.g., basic and continuing education or other capacity building programs) for developing the core skills needed for police to promote the rule of law and protect the population?** Two commissioned papers and a public workshop, called forth by the committee to address these questions, served as the primary sources of information for the committee's deliberations.

The committee's organizing framework for its review, described extensively in the committee's first report,[1] stems from an evidence-based approach to policing. Evidence-based policing is an approach to police practice and management that involves using scientifically derived knowledge to strengthen police departments' decision-making, tactics, strategies, and overall agency functioning. To promote the rule of law and protect the population, an evidence-based policing approach requires: (1) a reliable body of knowledge about myriad police practices for both contact with the public and internal operations; (2) the ongoing practice of targeting, testing, and tracking of police resources for achieving legitimate outcomes; and (3) the institutionalization and implementation of knowledge into police practices.

The committee recognizes the inherent challenge of its charge: the unknown extent to which knowledge primarily developed in the Global

---

[1] The committee's first report, *Policing to Promote the Rule of Law and Protect the Population: An Evidence-based Approach*, is available for download at https://www.nap.edu/26217.

North (mostly in the United States, United Kingdom, and Australia) can be generalized to police practices in the Global South and within different cultural, economic, educational, political, and social environments and contexts. Such differences can alter both the implementation and the impact of practices tested in one context and applied in another. What this report offers is a starting point toward developing stronger knowledge about how overseas assistance can help improve training outcomes for police institutions in these varied contexts.

REFORM-BASED TRAINING

In considering its broader charge and the landscape of policing reform, the committee notes that training alone cannot undo or repair a culture of mistrust or corruption in a government or police institution. If training is decoupled from other core elements of police institutions, its effects can be minimal—or worse, they can be detrimental, as when trainees see that what they are taught is not consistent with the strategy, systems, and processes in place. Training effects on a police agency's performance always depend on how training is articulated and coordinated with other institutional elements.

The committee identified this issue as the difference between "reform-based training" and "training-based reform" (see Chapter 2). The committee believes that much of the training supported by donor nations and in the Global North constitutes training-based reform, which uses training as the primary aspiration for seeking change. Training-based reforms are often provided in isolation from other policies or organizational adjustments that could limit or enhance the impact of the training. Reform-based training begins with the specific reform that is sought, and then considers all elements needed to achieve that reform, including creating or redefining units or appointing new leaders in an agency, changing organizational tasks, priorities, incentives, and strategies, strengthening management and accountability within a police organization, providing new technologies, creating partnerships with local community groups, and winning political support in the national legislature or from civil servants in key ministries. Such reform planning would address what training is needed to support such reform efforts. New approaches to training therefore need to be launched in concordance with improvements to other organizational systems to reinforce and sustain a new direction for policing improvement. Reform-based training emphasizes that training alone is not enough to ensure reform.

CONCLUSION 1: Training needs to be launched in concordance with other organizational systems to reinforce its message, so that it becomes

part of a comprehensive policing transformation, including changes to incentive, accountability, supervisory, and deployment structures that support training goals.

FIVE PRINCIPLES OF TRAINING

The evidence-based policing anchor of the committee's work provides a framework for reform-based training. Specifically, the committee reached a consensus on five connected principles of police training that are grounded in an evidence-based approach and that can support the rule of law and the protection of the public. These principles, which are interconnected, are:

1. *Training must do no harm.* Training must not only focus on the evidence about what is effective in protecting the public and promoting the rule of law, but it also must not contribute to negative consequences, abuses, or harms. The uses of training must be monitored for positive outcomes, negative consequences, and misuses. The remaining principles operationalize this goal.
2. *The content of training should be based on good evidence to the extent possible.* The policing strategies, tactics, knowledge, and skills that officers are trained on should be supported by evidence showing that they are effectively linked to supporting the rule of law and protecting the public. Both existing scientific knowledge and scientific approaches can help identify effective policing strategies and activities that officers should be trained upon.
3. *Training must also use evidence-based methods.* The educational methods of delivering training should also be selected based on evidence of impact. Finding effective ways for officers to learn, apply knowledge, and update that knowledge is essential in linking training to everyday practices, behaviors, and outcomes.
4. Police agencies must *continuously gather new evidence about the impact of training* content and methods by tracking, testing, and evaluating ongoing training efforts for implementation and outcomes.
5. *The delivery of training needs to be flexible and contextualized,* given the resources, cultures, and capacities of different police agencies that INL supports.

CONCLUSION 2: An evidence-based approach to police training emphasizes five principles: that training should do no harm; that training activities, tactics, and strategies should be supported by good evidence; that the educational training methods used are also effective; that organizations continuously track, test, and evaluate training efforts; and that the delivery of training needs to be flexible and contextualized.

EVIDENCE-BASED KNOWLEDGE AND SKILLS FOR POLICE TRAINING

The committee recognizes that basic and ongoing training are critically important for police officers, given the varied demands, stress, and specialized tasks of the profession. In this report, the committee does not attempt to assess all of the work demands, tasks, and requirements necessary to carry out the essential responsibilities of policing. Instead, it focuses on what is currently often absent in training that is likely to help achieve the goal of promoting the rule of law and protecting the population. Often absent from police training—including in the Global North—is scientific knowledge about effective policing strategies and tactics, empirical facts about crime, victimization, and offending, and theoretical approaches that can help officers think more critically about their everyday work. Many recruit training courses teach how to march, write reports, physically detain someone, and/or use vehicles and/or weapons. Yet these skills play a very minor role in protecting the public and promoting the rule of law. Police training must incorporate knowledge derived from the science of policing.

For example, empirical facts and well-accepted theories of crime and victimization from criminology can provide the foundational knowledge necessary for police officers to make more informed decisions about crime, offenders, and victims. Drawn from decades of scientific evidence about crime and the prevention of crime, these facts and theories not only form the building blocks of police strategies that are now known to be effective at reducing crime, but can also inform policies, strategies, and everyday police actions that better protect the public from harm. Key facts from science include these:

- *Crime concentrates in a small fraction of all places:* Recognizing this criminological fact means that police can target (and conserve) resources better by focusing their problem-solving attention on places that account for the most crimes and crime harm.
- *Crime concentrates at certain times of the day and days of the week:* Allocating police to the right places (hot spots) at the right times (hot times) and on the right days (hot days) improves police effectiveness at preventing crime.
- *Crime concentrates among few offenders:* A large proportion of crime is committed by a small proportion of all offenders who chronically display a wide range of offending behavior, with offenders who create the highest harm often committing fewer crimes than the high-frequency offenders who contribute to less overall harm.
- *Youthful offenders are likely to desist over time:* The vast majority of juveniles who commit minor offenses desist as they become

adults. Police can safely divert from prosecution low-level offending by most young people, since most will stop offending regardless.
- *Crime concentrates among repeat victims:* Repeat victimization is a pattern by which a small percentage of victims suffers a large percentage of all criminal victimization, and an even greater proportion of all crime harm.

Criminological theories also help police understand the mechanisms that create crime problems. They offer insight into how interventions might disrupt the conditions that create crime opportunities and can support an officer's more critical and problem-solving approach to dealing with crime problems. Four key theories of crime causation that are supported by extensive multinational research evidence have substantial relevance to policing:

1. *Routine Activities Theory:* Crime emerges when a likely offender converges with a suitable crime target in the absence of a capable guardian. Understanding people's everyday routines and the interaction between these routines and the opportunities for crime at specific places can help officers understand *why* crime concentrates at certain places and times.
2. *General Deterrence Theory:* Crime is reduced in populations that see continuing evidence of police presence and capacity to apprehend offenders; crime rises sharply when that capacity is sharply reduced (for example, in police strikes, or when police ignore crime-prone places).
3. *Residual Deterrence Theory:* Short periods of police presence in crime hot spots applied in intermittent and unpredictable ways can lead to longer periods without crime or disorder after police leave, not only at the immediate location of patrol but also in the surrounding vicinity.
4. *No Evidence of Immediate Spatial Displacement:* Police agencies often argue that by targeting particular places, times, and people within those place and times, that crime will simply "move around the corner" and be displaced. Robust evidence indicates that displacement is not common, and that surrounding areas are more likely to see a diffusion of benefits, when police target specific crime hot spots.

CONCLUSION 3: Training on the causes and patterns of crime (and antisocial behavior), rule of law, and human rights is needed in both recruit training and advanced training of police. Such training includes a foundation of criminological theories and empirical facts that develop

an understanding of how and why crime concentrates among certain offenders, places, times, and victims.

In addition to this knowledge about crime, offending, and victimization, training also needs to include the extensive knowledge that is now available from evaluation research in criminology on effective approaches to prevent crime, protect the public, reduce harm, and improve the ability for the police to support the rule of law. This knowledge has been extensively reviewed in two National Academies consensus studies: *Fairness and Effectiveness in Policing* and *Proactive Policing: Effects on Crime and Communities*.[2] There is scientific consensus on several policing approaches that they can be appropriately adjusted to varying policing contexts to reduce crime and improve police-citizen relationships. These findings suggest that the following are effective approaches (see Chapter 3):

- Targeting high-risk micro-geographic places or "hot spots" of crime, especially using problem-solving approaches;
- Focused deterrence strategies for high-risk offenders;
- Diversion for low-risk and youthful offenders;
- Risk assessment and protection orders to protect domestic violence victims from further abuse; and
- Spatial targeting of high-risk drug offenders within the drug market environment.

CONCLUSION 4: Officers must be trained on tactics, strategies, and actions that have been shown through high-quality research to effectively promote the rule of law and protect the public.

Science-based training on the causes and patterns of crime and on effective crime prevention approaches can complement ethics-based training on the rule of law and human rights. Training that links both helps to achieve Principle 1, that training should do no harm.

CONCLUSION 5: Training on the consequences of violating the rule of law and human rights principles can help police understand the role they play within society and the degradation that may occur to their authority when they abuse their power or fail to control police torture and corruption.

---

[2] These reports are available through the National Academies Press at https://www.nap.edu/catalog/10419/fairness-and-effectiveness-in-policing-the-evidence and https://www.nap.edu/catalog/24928/proactive-policing-effects-on-crime-and-communities.

In addition to knowledge about crime and effective policing approaches, several skills are needed to facilitate translating this knowledge into effective policing strategies and tactics that can advance the rule of law and protect the public simultaneously (see Chapter 3). These skills include:

- *Interacting with the public:* Interacting with diverse populations exercising cultural respect and with an awareness of one's own implicit and explicit biases.
- *Critical thinking skills:* Policing approaches that use problem-oriented policing, proactivity and crime analysis, community- and citizen-centric approaches, or geographic targeting require critical and creative thinking skills to integrate the knowledge described above into everyday activities.
- *Data skills:* A problem-solving approach requires officers to make decisions based on data and, more importantly, on data that are appropriately collected, collated, and analyzed as to be accurate.
- *Collaborating and building multi-agency partnerships:* A central part of police work is working in partnership with other agencies and entities to regulate, control, and prevent crime. Police need the skills necessary to work with local and government partners in providing integrated services to the different types of adults and youth with whom they come into contact.

CONCLUSION 6: Training is essential on skills for interacting with the public, and for problem-solving with partnerships for proactive responses guided by critical thinking and data analysis. Police training that includes content and analysis of routine data collection is likely to help police better identify and prioritize high-risk people, places, and vulnerable victims.

EFFECTIVE TRAINING METHODS AND DELIVERY

Training not only needs to focus on effective policing approaches to promote the rule of law and protect the population, it also needs to use effective educational methods and pedagogy. Effective teaching methods are essential to ensure that topics that officers and organizations are trained on will be maintained in officers' minds and then sustained and operationalized in practice. A central conclusion of the committee is that the way police officers are trained likely matters as much as the skills and knowledge on which they are trained.

While little rigorous evaluation has been conducted on training methods in the policing context, a number of best practice principles for training design and adult learning are available through the work of both researchers and industries. Generally, effective training is developed through a systematic process that includes conducting a training needs analysis, developing training objectives, selecting methods of training, pilot testing the training design, and evaluating the outcomes of training. From a reform-based training ideal, each of these steps would be connected to broader organizational changes. Additionally, these fundamental steps of training design apply to all levels of trainees from entry-level to management as well as instructors themselves in which training is aimed at preparing future instructors.

Existing evidence on adult learning pedagogy in the context of policing across various contexts and countries lends some advice for foreign assistance programs (see Chapter 4). First, the settings for police training are not just in a basic academy or in donor-sponsored training sessions but occur in formal "field training" or "in-service training" and informal settings such as everyday supervision and mentorship in the field. Each provides unique opportunities for training and also obstacles to training that developers and trainers should consider when designing training goals and curricula. Second, and specific to policing, training using problem-based learning methods, scenario-based training, and training that develops critical thinking skills seems most appropriate, given both the complexities of policing and the knowledge base that is needed for effective policing, as discussed above.

Third, close attention has to be paid to who is providing training. The trustworthiness of agency leadership and instructors appears to influence training outcomes as well as the type of learning method selected by the trainer. In addition, specific behaviors of trainers influence training outcomes. Field training officers are thought to play a critical role in socializing officers by demonstrating and reinforcing police agency and community values outside the police academy setting. However, these factors may also work against training goals if trusted instructors are not teaching the correct content. Instructors must also have a strong knowledge of the facts and theories of crime as well as the knowledge base on effective strategies to protect the public and ensure the rule of law. Additionally, this knowledge of crime and prevention must be contextualized within the local context. Thus, using local trainers who have appropriate general education may offer a means to train those trainers at a regional level. Training designs may be bolstered by including local police in curriculum development and evaluation of training. This could ensure that police agencies are aware of how to find scientifically validated research and how to translate that research into accessible curriculum for trainees. Plans that include an evaluation component, ideally one with a credible causal design, need to be prioritized when at all possible.

CONCLUSION 7: Given the lack of research on teaching effectiveness in the policing context, implementation of promising methods should be evaluated to confirm whether they support officer learning and use of knowledge and skills in practice. Finding effective ways to train police officers, with knowledgeable and respected instructors, using experiential and problem-oriented approaches is key to advancing reform-based training from an evidence-based policing perspective.

TRACKING, TESTING, AND EVALUATING TRAINING

The committee finds that the body of evidence on outcomes from different training content or methods is substantially underdeveloped. In particular, the documentation of training implementation, the quality and nature of training across different instructors or modalities, and the connection between training and outcomes in the field are rarely tracked. The committee's consensus is that investments in evaluation of police training are likely to increase police capacity to promote the rule of law and protect the population. Popularly promoted and frequently used training programs (e.g., de-escalation, procedural justice, implicit bias training, and community-oriented policing) remain underevaluated all over the world.

In order to answer critical questions of training effectiveness, rigorous evaluations of police training outcomes must occur prior to, or at least in concert with, widespread promotion and implementation of any training programs. The ongoing accumulation of knowledge of how people learn as well as innovations in learning tools and technologies require institutions to assess continually how training is conducted.

Given the massive expenditure on training by INL and other donor nations, a need for tracking, testing, and evaluating training against specific outcomes is required to ensure that the achievement of sought-after goals is met. Individual countries receiving funds from INL can also assist by being required to keep track of the uses of training content, the continuation or dissemination of training to others, or results of training implementation against specific outcomes.

1

Introduction

Police departments train both new recruits and seasoned veterans to help shape how police officers do their jobs. Recruits are enrolled in basic training with the hope that they will acquire both the knowledge and the skills necessary to meet the expectations of their profession. Veteran officers may return to training while "in service" to refresh their knowledge or learn new skills. Less often, newly promoted supervisors and senior leaders receive specialized training in management or supervision or in specific areas of expertise that they are expected to pass along to those they supervise.

Foreign assistance donor organizations, like the U.S. State Department's Bureau of International Narcotics and Law Enforcement Affairs (INL),[1] provide training to police officers as part of their assistance efforts overseas. Such training has varied in form and dosage. It covers a range of purposes: demonstrating police tactics, sharing community-oriented policing practices, developing managerial skills in senior officers, preparing front-line officers for specific deployment, and building greater training capacity within a country. Where possible, INL aims to provide training from the top, focused on senior leadership, down through managers, supervisors, and then entry-level personnel to ensure that all levels are prepared to employ as well as support the use of essential knowledge and skills (U.S. Department of State, 2016).

---

[1] The mission of INL is to help "partner governments assess, build, reform, and sustain competent and legitimate criminal justice systems, and [develop and implement] the architecture necessary for international drug control and cross-border law enforcement cooperation." See https://www.state.gov/about-us-bureau-of-international-narcotics-and-law-enforcement-affairs/.

Training programs can be an important mechanism in donor nations' efforts to reform and develop police organizations around the globe. Ensuring a return on investment from these efforts requires attention to training effectiveness and the sustainability of the knowledge and skill transfers from such training. As discussed in this report, a central goal for police training is to transfer the knowledge and skills necessary for police to promote the rule of law and protect the population (see Box 1-1 for the committee's perspective on rule of law and protection of the population).

THE COMMITTEE'S CHARGE

The National Academies of Sciences, Engineering, and Medicine assembled the Committee on Evidence to Advance Reform in the Global Security and Justice Sectors ("the committee") to identify the best available research evidence on how police reform can promote the rule of law (including human rights) and protect the public. The committee comprises experts in criminology, economics, international and organized crime, law, policing, and political science and brings knowledge and experience from a portfolio of work that spans four continents. Such experience includes conducting research as well as advising governments on police policy in several countries including but not limited to Afghanistan, Brazil, Colombia, Ghana, India, South Korea, the United Kingdom, and the United States (see the Appendix for more details).

The committee was charged with producing a series of five reports, each addressing areas of interest to INL (see Box 1-2). To assist with this assignment, the committee developed a series of five public information-gathering sessions to bring together researchers and practitioners with experience in each subtopic to be examined. This report is the second in the series, addressing the second question in the committee's charge:

> What are the core knowledge and skills needed for police to promote the rule of law and protect the population? What is known about mechanisms (e.g., basic and continuing education or other capacity building programs) for developing the core skills needed for police to promote the rule of law and protect the population?[2]

Approach to the Study

Like the others in the series, this report reflects the development of consensus advice to address the questions in the charge. The committee

---

[2]Each consensus report in the series of five reports will be released as a PDF in sequence of completion.

BOX 1-1
Rule of Law and Protection of the Population

For the purpose of its study, the committee leverages definitions of the rule of law (ROL) from the United Nations and the U.S. State Department. Neyroud (2021) offers a thorough discussion of the challenges in defining the ROL. Several sources provide succinct definitions of ROL. For example, the United Nations defines it as

> A principle of governance in which all persons, institutions, and entities, public and private, including the state itself, are accountable to laws that are publicly promulgated, equally enforced, and independently adjudicated that are consistent with international human rights norms and standards. It requires measures to ensure adherence to the principles of supremacy of law, equality before the law, accountability to the law, fairness in the application of the law, separation of powers, participation in decision-making, legal certainty, avoidance of arbitrariness, and procedural and legal transparency.[a]

The U.S. State Department's Bureau of International Narcotics and Law Enforcement Affairs defines the concept as:

> A principle of governance in which all persons, institutions, and entities, public, and private, including the state itself, are accountable to [domestic] laws that are publicly promulgated, equally enforced, and independently adjudicated, that are consistent with international human rights norms and standards.[b]

Other dimensions and detailed conditions of the ROL are available in the broad legal and philosophical literature (e.g., Bingham, 2011; O'Donnell, 2004). From a scientific perspective, the committee's primary concern is how any definition of ROL is empirically measured. Given its complexity, ROL is likely to vary in degree both across countries and within them over time. That feature has generated a range of cross-country measures for the ROL (Cheung, 2019; Rajah, 2012; Versteeg and Ginsburg, 2017), each of which tends to observe the kinds of features found in the existing codes of human rights and policing practice promoted by international agencies.

A fundamental component of the rule of law is that the state itself be held accountable to the law. As such, the police institution has great responsibility to act in ways consistent with laws and international human rights norms and standards. Adherence to human rights standards, understood as a set of normative commitments (Bottoms and Tankebe, 2017), is related to increased legitimacy in policing, including aspects such as restraining from the abuse of force and providing safety to the citizens to ensure that they can exercise their rights and obligations.

[a] https://www.un.org/ruleoflaw/what-is-the-rule-of-law/.
[b] https://www.state.gov/wp-content/uploads/2019/03/222048.pdf.

SOURCE: NASEM, 2021, pp. 18–19.

BOX 1-2
Statement of Task

An ad hoc committee of the National Academies of Sciences, Engineering, and Medicine will consider evidence in the areas of policing institutions, police practices and capacities, and police legitimacy in the international context. The committee will hold a series of five public workshops; each of the workshops will focus on a targeted set of questions of interest to the State Department and serve as the primary data source for a brief consensus report. Drawing on relevant literature, particularly from the international context, the project will inform the State Department's capacity-building activities aimed at strengthening the effectiveness of local, in-country law enforcement agencies, building the technical skills of foreign law enforcement personnel through training and technical assistance, and assisting in institutional police reform at the local level.

Each of the five workshops will bring together experts to discuss the evidence and its implications for the international sector, as well as practitioners using the evidence to implement policy. Some papers may be commissioned for one or more workshops. The committee will issue brief independent consensus reports after each public workshop. These reports will include conclusions and recommendations as appropriate and provide practical guidance on key implications of the evidence for the field.

1. What organizational policies, structures, or practices (e.g., HR and recruiting, legal authorities, reporting lines, etc.) enable a police service to promote the rule of law and protect the population?
2. **What are the core knowledge and skills needed for police to promote the rule of law and protect the population? What is known about mechanisms (e.g., basic and continuing education or other capacity building programs) for developing the core skills needed for police to promote the rule of law and protect the population?**
3. What policies and practices for police use of force are effective in promoting the rule of law and protecting the population (including officers themselves)? What is known about effective practices for implementing those policies and practices in recruitment, training, and internal affairs?
4. What policing practices build community trust and legitimacy in countries with low-to-moderate criminal justice sector capacity?
5. What are the systemic features needed to effectively control high-level corruption, and how can police effectively contribute to efforts to combat high-level corruption?

was tasked to carry out the entire study within a year and a half and to release each of the five reports separately and sequentially during this time period. In forming its advice, the committee draws specifically on information from prepared papers and a single workshop on the topic of the second question as well as its years of experience investigating policing policies and practices.

The public workshop entitled *Assessing International Police Training to Promote the Rule of Law and Protect the Population*, held virtually on May 24 and 27, 2021, was designed to gather information on the state of research evidence around police training. Workshop participants included members of the committee, representatives from INL, and international researchers and practitioners in police training and development. An effort was made to assemble a diverse set of participants who work with and study policing in several different contexts such as those in Africa, Australia, Latin America, the Middle East, and the United States.

The workshop discussions were framed around commissioned papers prepared by Lorraine Mazerolle, The University of Queensland, Australia, and Tamara Herold, University of Nevada, Las Vegas. The Mazerolle paper provided an assessment of the existing evidence supporting the core knowledge and skills that need to be included in police academy training to promote the ROL and the protection of the public. The Herold paper examined existing training methodologies deployed in support of training curricula. Both papers assessed the strengths and limitations of the evidence and data for these practices. The committee relied on the assessments and analyses presented in the papers to inform its deliberations and draws heavily from them throughout this report.[3]

The workshop examined what is known, unknown, or untested regarding police training internationally, as delivered both in-country in police classroom settings for new recruits and in-service officers and during the ad hoc training opportunities provided by members of the international donor community in and outside of recipient countries. Workshop panelists were invited from the United Nations Office on Drugs and Crime, the U.S. Department of Justice International Criminal Investigative Training Assistance Program, the Nigerian Police Force, and academic institutions with expertise in researching these themes and experience in designing and delivering police training. Discussions at the workshop, including those about the commissioned papers, were a primary source of information for the committee's deliberations. Speakers were identified based on the relevance of their work to the study question.

After the workshop, the committee met three times virtually over a period of two months to deliberate on what it learned from the papers and

---

[3] The commissioned papers are available on the project website.

heard at the workshop in order to reach a consensus on conclusions and recommendations for its report. The committee's draft report was subsequently reviewed by a set of similar subject matter experts and revised in response to review in accordance with National Academies' procedures before being finalized for release.

The report presents the committee's assessment of the information it has gathered and provides guidance for police training based on the state of research evidence in this area. It does not contain complete workshop proceedings, but instead draws on resources and descriptions from the workshop discussion as relevant.[4]

As a project commissioned to conduct five workshops and produce five reports in a rapid production process, the committee's methods differ somewhat from the single consensus report model, such as the report recently prepared by the ad hoc consensus committee on proactive policing (see NASEM, 2018c). The breadth of the current assignment and the speed with which it was required led the committee to rely more on its pre-existing knowledge of the research findings than on systematic reviewing of all available studies—even as new research was published while the project was underway.

The Committee's Interpretation of Its Charge

The committee recognizes that basic, entry-level training and ongoing training are crucial for police officers, given the varied demands, stress, and specialized tasks of the profession. In this report, the committee does not attempt to assess all of the work demands, tasks, and requirements necessary to carry out the essential responsibilities of policing. Instead, it focuses on what is currently often absent in training that is likely to be productive toward promoting the rule of law and protecting the population.

As discussed in Chapter 2, the committee emphasizes that training should only be considered one part of any reform effort. What makes police organizations successful at promoting the ROL and protecting the population will depend on how well training is integrated with organizational policies, systems, and incentives that are also aimed at the goal of promoting the rule of law and protecting the population.

The committee acknowledges the complex challenges of translating knowledge from research into "what works" in the Global North into police reform in the Global South. While the study of policing outcomes

---

[4]Full recordings of the workshop are available at https://www.nationalacademies.org/event/05-27-2021/evidence-to-advance-reform-in-the-global-security-and-justice-sectors-workshop-2-public-session-1 and https://www.nationalacademies.org/event/05-27-2021/evidence-to-advance-reform-in-the-global-security-and-justice-sectors-workshop-2-public-session-2.

has increased in recent years, it still remains limited in context, with much of the research conducted on policing taking place in the Global North[5] (e.g., the United Kingdom, United States, and Australia). Such studies also are limited in purpose, with much research focused on examining changes to the crime rate instead of examining the harms to the public as the result of crimes, violence, and any consequences of policing activities. Real impediments to transferring what is known about policing from one context to another can include "differences in cultures and language, political regimes, legal systems, and the extent of political corruption" (NASEM, 2021, p. 2).

Nonetheless, this report is written with the premise that there is an opportunity in many global contexts to build on existing evidence. Digesting that evidence can help to generate new knowledge aimed at promoting the rule of law and protection of the population. This opportunity is afforded by an evidence-based approach to policing and policing reform. The committee details the framework for evidence-based policing in its first report (NASEM, 2021) and identifies, in this report, five principles from that framework for training. In the committee's opinion, following these principles to shape, implement, and evaluate police training will be productive toward transforming not only police training but ultimately policing.

EVIDENCE-BASED POLICING: FIVE PRINCIPLES FOR TRAINING

As described extensively in the committee's first report (NASEM, 2021), the committee's organizing framework stems from an evidence-based approach to policing. Evidence-based policing (EBP) is an approach to police practice and management that uses scientifically derived information to strengthen police departments' decision-making, tactics, strategies, and overall agency functioning. An EBP approach requires a reliable body of knowledge about myriad police practices for both internal organization and external activities; the ongoing practice of targeting, testing, and tracking these activities against legitimate outcomes; and the institutionalization and implementation of knowledge in police practices (Lum and Koper, 2017; Sherman, 1998, 2013).

An evidence-based conceptual framework suggests five principles for training. These principles are:

1. Ensuring that training does no harm;
2. Selecting training *content* by relying on (and translating from) what is known about effective policing from police science;

---

[5]The terms Global North and Global South have come to label countries along socio-economic and political characteristics and less so on geographical positions.

3. Deploying training methods that have been scientifically tested for successful training outcomes;
4. Continuously gathering new evidence to test and track ongoing training for outcomes in each training institution; and
5. Delivering training in ways that are flexible and contextualized.

As with an evidence-based approach to policing as discussed in the committee's first report (NASEM, 2021), these principles are not often used by leaders to guide police training. The majority of basic training programs, both globally and within the United States, have focused on performing specific tasks, rather than on integrating scientifically based knowledge about effective policing into a wide range of activities that improve cognitive and decision-making abilities (Bradford and Pynes, 1999).

The first principle of an evidence-based conceptual framework for training is that police agencies need to implement training with an emphasis on the fundamental theory that police must do no harm. Training must not only focus on the evidence about what is effective in protecting the public and promoting the ROL, but it also must not contribute to negative consequences, abuses, or harms. The uses of training must be monitored for positive outcomes, negative consequences, and misuses. The remaining principles operationalize this goal.

The second principle is the need to train officers by *translating* what is known from science about crime and crime prevention into their policing practice and activities. Some of this knowledge is summarized in the committee's first report (NASEM, 2021) and is discussed here with specific reference to training in Chapter 3. While this may seem to be an obvious first principle, police agencies in both the Global North and the Global South continue to *not* focus on this knowledge. Instead, a great deal of time in police training is devoted to standard operating procedures, such as writing reports, submitting forensic evidence, and making arrests. Routine symbolic activities, such as marching, saluting, shoe-shining, and uniform-wearing, and technical skills, such as driving, shooting, running, and jumping, also consume substantial time. Lum and Koper (2017) note a typical consequence of this procedures-based approach: while agencies often spend a great deal of time teaching officers how to get from point A to point B they spend very little, if any, time training officers to understand how and why crime is clustered at point C and what to do about that clustering.

The third principle emphasizes that decisions about *how officers are taught* should be based in sound evidence about effective learning in policing. For example: Are classroom lectures less or more effective than field training at developing specific skills? Can skills-based practicing and problem-solving exercises help to institutionalize evidence into practice? Will repetition, coaching, or mentoring by supervisors help build receptivity to this knowledge? This principle asserts that curricula should be taught using the best educational approaches for adult learners (see Chapter 4). Lecture-based learning in a classroom may not be the most effective mode of education for many critical policing skills (for example, communication skills for successful citizen interactions or analytical skills for solving recurrent problems). Decisions about how officers are taught can also include instructional "scaffolding" combined with experiential learning opportunities. Scaffolding is a process through which instruction or police training units enhance officer learning by systematically building on students' experiences and knowledge as they acquire new skills. For example, knowledge learned in the classroom might be better translated into practice if that knowledge is coupled with practical exercises and/or reinforced through field supervision that encourages the use of training in practice. Training effectiveness may also vary across context and country, depending on the organizational infrastructure and resources available for training.

The fourth principle of an evidence-based framework for training requires *ongoing testing and tracking* of the training to ensure that it is connected with changes in officer behavior and outcomes (Sherman, 2013). The practice of EBP requires that agencies—including those like INL that are involved in promoting policing reform—actively and consistently account for, assess, and evaluate their practices against consistent standards, knowledge about effective police practices, and effective training approaches. This requires aligning their efforts with current knowledge about policing and actively testing and evaluating their practices to determine whether they achieve the sought-after outcomes (Sherman, 1998). It also requires ongoing evaluation of training content to determine whether it has been correctly translated into practice in ways that lead to those outcomes. Testing and tracking are also important components of police accountability—ensuring that officers are carrying out duties as trained and expected.

The fifth principle of an evidence-based framework for training requires that the delivery of training needs to be flexible and contextualized, given the resources, cultures, and capacities of different police agencies that INL supports. For example, police agencies looking to adopt training that has been proven effective elsewhere might face legal (e.g., limits on officer discretion) or financial (e.g., lack of funding) obstacles unique to their own national or local governing structures and resources. Moreover, understanding the context-specific forces that drive crime and violence in specific regions or countries and adapting training to be relevant to those factors is important (Ratcliffe, 2016).[6] There can also be cultural differences in societal expectations, perceptions of police, and differences in local customs and norms that affect how a specific form of police training will impact officers and communities. Assessment of these contextual differences and efforts to cultivate necessary implementation conditions should precede or be coupled with attempts to develop appropriate police training.

ORGANIZATION OF THE REPORT

The committee's aim for this report is to provide guidance to INL and other foreign assistance donors as they work to improve and incorporate knowledge from science into their training programs. The five principles for training presented in this chapter and the framework for EBP from its first report (NASEM, 2021) guided the committee's review of the findings and training needs presented to them. Following this introduction, Chapter 2 presents the committee's perspective on reform-based training. Chapter 3 outlines the core knowledge and skills police need to promote the ROL and protect the population, drawing heavily from commissioned work from Lorraine Mazerolle (2021). Chapter 4 draws from work presented by Tamara Herold (2021) to the committee and examines the training environment, including teaching methods and instructors, and a set of evaluations deployed within police academies designed to assess the effects of different methods. Chapter 5 outlines key implications from the scientific literature for police training. The Appendix provides biographical sketches of committee members and study staff.

---

[6] In a survey of officers from seven Central American countries, Ratcliffe (2016) found some regional commonalities but also significant local variation in numerous characteristics perceived by law enforcement as successful characteristics of gangs. The different nuances that emerged across countries suggest the importance of adaptability of training, especially when exporting training from the Global North to the Global South. Taking perspectives and priorities from officers in the Global North related to gang violence could lead to trainings that focus on areas that are of little value in understanding the situation in Honduras or El Salvador, for example.

2

Reform-based Training

The committee makes a distinction between *training-based reform* and *reform-based training*. It also recognizes the challenges of institutional and political barriers to the administration of training.

TRAINING-BASED REFORM

For over half a century, Global North nations including the United Kingdom and the United States have sought to reform police agencies in the Global South using what the committee considers an approach of training-based reforms. This approach views training as the primary vehicle by which the rule of law and protection of the public can be promoted. Training-based reforms also reflect a common policing philosophy in the Global North: that by providing training, the agency absolves itself of responsibility if an officer does something wrong post-training. However, training has not been clearly connected to a specific change in policing, a broader vision of agency reform, or even a wider change in local or national governance. Part of the reason for this is that police agencies have not used a framework—such as evidence-based policing—for testing whether training succeeded in producing intended reforms. Instead, the fact that training was delivered was itself the measure of success.[1]

---

[1] A poignant example of this lack of a link between training and outcomes is the case of Derek Chauvin, the Minneapolis officer who killed George Floyd. At the time Chauvin killed Floyd, the Minneapolis Police Department (and Chauvin) had been up to date with very progressive training on implicit bias, use of force, procedural justice, and community policing.

One reason training-based reform has not been tested or tracked for success is that the purpose and goals of training can be numerous, highly diffuse, or not even agreed upon by police leadership or the community. For example, is the aim of training in firearms to protect the officer, to protect the community, or to satisfy the legal liability concerns of officers carrying guns? Are officers trained in diversity issues and implicit bias to improve internal diversity in the force, reduce prejudice and biased behavior toward the community, or simply to allow officers to acknowledge their own biases?

A sober assessment of this approach suggests that training alone cannot accomplish what a state has failed to achieve in other respects. There is little evidence, for example, that training alone can control corruption in government generally, get officers to take actions to prevent crime or safeguard the public, dismantle organized crime groups, or resist insurgency attacks on police stations. Nevertheless, there may be reasons to believe that police training can play an important role in accomplishing these and other worthy goals, though doing so may require a new approach of how training relates to reform.

REFORM-BASED TRAINING

The idea of *reform-based training* proposes a different approach. It first asks, what specific reform should be accomplished in the ways the agency delivers police services? Second, what are all the steps needed to achieve the reform, including creating new units or appointing leaders, providing new technologies, creating partnerships with local community groups, and winning political support in the national legislature or from civil servants in key ministries? Then, only after these questions are answered, the reform plan would address this question: what training is needed to support such reform efforts?

As an example, consider the problem of illegal land seizures, in which large companies clear wild forest lands for mining or growing cash crops. Local police may be legally entitled to stop them, but corruption and threats of violence against police discourage actions against such developers. Reform-based training could be a part of the solution, along with a plan for special prosecutors and investigators to seize the assets of illegal developers, with support from a national ministry of justice or interior. In this scenario, the training would teach a new procedure for local police to follow as soon as such illegal development is discovered.

Another example might be the inconsistent use of arrest or force on individuals from different racial or ethnic groups. If the reform sought is a

---

And yet, Chavin still killed Floyd while other officers stood by without stopping him (Bella et al., 2021).

reduction in disparities in police actions toward the public (that is, pursuing equal protection of the laws), achieving this reform requires not only that officers be trained in how their actions contribute to bias (and ways they can mitigate those behaviors). It also requires supervisory and accountability systems to be put in place to regularly monitor officer behaviors and coach them to adjust their behavior to be aligned with the training they have received. Agencies might also have to discard certain operations that conflict with the goals of training—in this case, operations that continue to result in disparities in police action toward the public (for example, indiscriminate stop-and-frisks or traffic stops).

Evaluating such examples would thus go far beyond the question of whether training was delivered to all officers. Evaluations would include clearly describing the outcomes the agency is seeking before the training began. They would include evaluating the entire plan to achieve those reforms (with training making up only one part of the plan). Ensuring that training was effective would also require training supervisors in coaching, mentoring, and managing officers who have received training, to hold them accountable to new behaviors or activities. Finally, if the training was delivered, the evaluation would examine the effects of new police practices on the outcomes intended for those practices, such as reduced violence or racial disparity.

The committee recognizes that transitioning from training-based reforms to reform-based training could take many years and involve a deeper government and state commitment to reform. Yet there may be ready platforms for this approach in any annual reviews of the overall state of policing in a country receiving foreign donations. INL, for example, already has a yearly review process examining a full range of reform goals and concerns. That process may provide a prime opportunity to move from training-based reforms to reform-based training.

In the interim, there remain several crucial questions about the content and form of police training as part of foreign assistance efforts. Our discussion of those questions should not be seen as an endorsement of training-based reform. Instead, we address some of those questions as a kind of stopgap for doing the best that can be done with an existing approach to training, even while we would prefer to replace it.

POLITICS OF POLICE REFORM

Police reforms, including reforms of training programs, often face a range of obstacles or complicating factors. Some obstacles may come from resource constraints or technical challenges. Yet as much research suggests, the primary barriers to reform are political and institutional conditions both internal and external to the police agencies. Through quantitative studies in both democratic and electoral authoritarian countries, scholars have shown that electoral considerations can shape leaders' decisions regarding policing, including the enforcement of local laws (Holland, 2015) and the geographic distribution of officers (Hassan, 2017). Meanwhile, a growing literature, based mainly on qualitative case studies, has shown that political pressures, including scandals, can be a significant driver of police reforms (González, 2021; Sherman, 1978; Taylor, 2014; Ungar, 2002). At the same time, scholars have also shown that would-be police reformers may well have to contend with additional political factors that complicate reforms, including informal political rules (Sabet, 2012) and partisan competition, which can impede the adoption (Davis, 2006) and limit the durability of police reforms (Eaton, 2008; Hinton, 2006).

Although it is difficult to pinpoint the causal effect of political conditions and institutional characteristics, the social science literature suggests that these factors may play a role in shaping police reform inputs and outcomes, including training. In particular, research by Hernán Flom (2019) has shown that turnover between rival political parties can diminish the incentive to implement a predecessor's reform policy. In his presentation to the committee about his role as a practitioner charged with overseeing training for the Argentine Federal Police, Flom described how training programs were vulnerable to partisan turnover, undermining the continuity of training programs from one administration to the next (see Box 2-1).

CONCLUSION

The relationship between police training and governmental reform is an inherently political question. An obvious source of political conflict is the macro-level politics concerning which constituencies gain the most powerful and numerous police appointments in ethnically, culturally, or tribally diverse nations. This conflict can play a central role in deciding what kind of training police will receive.

In some countries, other kinds of politics may also be paramount. For example, tensions between permanent civil servants and newly elected members of parliaments may turn police training into a political football, with control over the policy going back and forth between those two groups and—perhaps—police professionals themselves. In other contexts, police officer unions, fraternal or other secret societies, or religious groups may play equally powerful roles in shaping training decisions, often with little transparency or rationale.

All these political dynamics of police training can pose complexity for foreign assistance donors. Commitments by one government to deliver a reform-based training program (or training-based reforms) may be de-emphasized by a new government, or opposed from the outset by national

BOX 2-1
Impact of Training on Police Institutions and Organizations (Workshop Presentation)

At the public information gathering session, speaker Hernán Flom, Trinity College and formerly of the National Ministry of Security in Argentina, stressed that training can positively impact certain aspects of police behavior and performance. Yet he also recognized that officers often learn more by doing their job rather than going through a formal training process. Flom reviewed the challenges of police training design and implementation from a political and policy perspective. He summarized the challenges by noting that politics is inseparable from police policies and that governmental support is integral to long-term, sustainable change.

Organizational Barriers

Drawing on his background with the National Security Ministry in Argentina from 2017 to 2019, Flom highlighted a key design challenge to reform-based training: a lack of strategic vision. While the Argentinian government had a broad model for the kind of police force it wanted, it had not defined the details related to police structure, function, and career tracks to achieve those reforms. This lack of vision was compounded by the desire to base their force on an inappropriate model—that of the Federal Bureau of Investigation (FBI) in the United States. Not only were there significant differences between the Argentinian and U.S. criminal justice systems, but there were also differences between the FBI and federal police in Argentina. In addition, there were also tensions in Argentina between politicians that promoted transformation, including changes in training, and police who were reluctant to accept it and between the newly arrived political authorities and bureaucratic staff who remained from previous administrations. Taken together, Flom explained that these factors made it difficult to define new core skills and competencies for a new police training curriculum, while also finding a good balance between the academic and practical contents.

Implementation Challenges

Flom also highlighted obstacles to implementing policing training. A notable obstacle, he said, is the lack of either human or budgetary resources. The Government of Argentina was short on technical bureaucratic staff, and political authorities often had to multitask between technical jobs and their political roles. Therefore, external consultants with different expertise and incentives were often brought in to fill in this gap. Flom also described a situation of fiscal austerity the last two years of the administration, so there were no resources to hire staff or update classrooms with proper technology for police training. A critical problem was a lack of coordination within the ministry itself. The lack of coordination had consequences: an overabundance of training because so many different groups within the ministry and across other federal forces were involved. That led to a burden of excess time and money on those attending. Time was another scarce resource, Flom noted. This made his team's work seem even more difficult

continued

> **BOX 2-1 Continued**
>
> because they needed to align their proposed training changes with political or electoral cycles and university calendars or police academy cycles. Finally, he highlighted the dilemma for a political administration between its control over the police and developing the necessary trust that fuels lasting changes, especially on issues such as training that require delegation to the police.
>
> NOTE: This speaker summary is presented as a factual accounting of what was presented at the workshop for the committee's consideration. The statements reflected here are those of the individual presenter and do not necessarily represent the views of all workshop participants or the committee.

civil servants who are in constant tension with police leaders. Given the dynamic and fragile nature of agreements, the specific aims of police training seem more likely to be accomplished if any politics of training itself is clear from the outset. A realistic approach to risk assessment, with a series of scenarios and fallback positions, could be informative. If the purpose of the training is to promote reform, a "pre-mortem" examination (Kahneman, 2011) of how the intervention might fail would be an appropriate precaution before any funding is transferred. Similarly, a series of compliance tests could be imposed, so that funding could halt soon after any evidence emerged of the training itself being subverted by a country's internal politics of police training.

A final point about the politics of police training is that it remains largely unexamined. It would be of great value to donors to fund new studies on these issues, comparing successful and unsuccessful assistance from the standpoint of whether funds were spent as planned, and if not, why not. A more systematic approach to documenting and assessing training assistance efforts, including some tracking of results or even receptivity to the training, would create a written, institutional body of knowledge for future police training.

3

Knowledge and Skills for Policing

The task of the committee was to address a fundamental question about police training: "what are the core knowledge and skills needed for police to promote the rule of law and protect the population?" As noted in Chapter 1, the second principle when applying an evidence-based conceptual framework to police training is that police agencies need to train officers by *translating into practice what is known from science.*

This chapter provides an overview of established science on crime that should be translated to knowledge and skills and included in the education and training of police officers and leaders to achieve the aims of promoting the rule of law (ROL) and protecting the population. All jurisdictions have specific laws and regulations that dictate the local powers of law enforcement officers that will be important for officers to learn, but those legal curricula are beyond the scope of this study. Likewise, there are numerous opportunities to build the knowledge and skills necessary to carry out procedures in one's agency and operate and use equipment, yet this chapter does not address these types of knowledge and skills. Our focus, instead, is on the foundational knowledge and skills that both are needed to promote fair, legal, and effective policing practices and can be integrated into a number of training programs. In the committee's view, based on its experiences with police training, much of this core knowledge is sorely absent from training curricula across countries in both the Global North and the Global South.

In summarizing the core content of knowledge that policing needs to apply, the chapter describes relevant facts and theory in the science of criminology, including the concentration of most crime into small percentages of all places, times, offenders, and victims, and related patterns of criminality.

The committee believes this knowledge is important for all levels of police officers (e.g., recruits, frontline, supervisors, management, and leadership) and those that become instructors of training programs. It recognizes that such knowledge may be integrated into curricula in different ways for different levels and serve different purposes. It is particularly important for training instructors to be well versed in criminological facts and theories so they can impart this knowledge appropriately in the context of training-specific tactics or strategies.

Likely this knowledge would be discussed at a basic level for recruit and frontline officers, with graduated levels of information and emphasis for supervisors, management, instructors, and leadership. Frontline officers may appreciate the facts about crime and how their efforts may be effective toward reducing crime or reducing the damages in response to crime. Supervisors and management may find the knowledge most useful for resource allocation as well as to inform their own efforts to support appropriate policing behaviors and outcomes in the community. The committee observed that training specifically for supervisors and their role in overseeing the use and sustainability of appropriate knowledge and skills is often lacking.

Before discussing scientific findings and the core knowledge useful for policing, we highlight our view on important supervisory skills. Later in the chapter, we expand on key skills for police organizations, informed by evidence-based approaches to policing, which are likely to be critical for promoting the rule of law and protecting the population but are currently underemphasized in police training.

The research literature and findings presented here are based on a paper prepared for the committee (Mazerolle, 2021). This paper drew on evidence captured in the Global Policing Database.[1] This database contains high-quality research studies of interventions related to policing, including training programs, from 87 countries. This chapter also draws upon the two National Academies reports on policing: *Fairness and Effectiveness in Policing: The Evidence* (NRC, 2004) and *Proactive Policing: Effects on Crime and Communities* (NASEM, 2018c). These two reports extensively review the research in policing about effective and fair interventions to

---

[1] The database is a web-based (https://gpd.uq.edu.au) exhaustive repository of intervention research relating to police and policing practices. The majority (n = 1822; 52.3%) of all eligible studies (quasi, randomized controlled trial, and systematic reviews) originate from the United States and the top 20 countries see a high prevalence of European work, especially from the United Kingdom (n = 241; 6.9%). Australia also has a high contribution to the database (n = 190 studies; 5.4%) while India (n = 42; 1.2%) is the only country outside of the Americas, Europe, or Oceania whose contribution status ranks in the top 10. Countries from Africa, Asia, South America, and the Middle East appear in the top 20, although they are underrepresented with less than one percent of the publications per country.

reduce and prevent crime and improve police legitimacy in the eyes of the public.

SUPERVISORY SKILLS

Police leaders and supervisors must be well versed in the knowledge base discussed below, perhaps even more so than officers and perhaps at a higher scaffold level than for officers. For example, while officers might be taught the basics about problem-solving or even theories of how crime patterns emerge (and what to do to address those patterns), first-line supervisors may need much more in-depth training on carrying out all steps of the suggested Scanning, Analysis, Response, and Assessment problem-solving model (Eck and Spelman, 1987). Supervisors may be the ones who have to scan and identify problems or even carry out the basic analysis to better understand them. They may be needed to guide officers in problem-solving or critical thinking and, therefore, they must know not only what officers are taught, but perhaps what trainers know when they are teaching officers.

Supervisors also need to be able to identify when officers deviate from their training. Traditional approaches to policing have used performance metrics that are not obviously aligned with this approach. For example, officers are frequently judged on how many arrests they make or how many calls they answer. However, more appropriate and aligned performance metrics must be developed to support supervisors in their management of officers in evidence-based approaches. The ways in which officers are incentivized and evaluated at all stages of their careers likely influence how they work. Supervisors will require training in judging whether officers are implementing the activities, actions, dispositions, and communication styles for a new, problem-solving approach. Taking this a step further, supervisors may need to be trained on how to effectively conduct daily observations and audits of what officers are doing, including training on the right inquiries that will help them determine what officers are doing (NASEM, 2021). They may need training on how to spend their time during the day to effectively balance their administrative duties with observing or auditing officers at the right times and situations. Some assessments of officer performance might also come from analytic sources that supervisors either have to interpret or create. Training on gathering, collating, and analyzing personnel activities or even crime data to better understand officer behavior is critical.

If supervisors are to ensure that officers implement the skills and knowledge they receive in training, the supervisors themselves may also need to be trained in coaching, mentorship, and leadership techniques. This will enable them to relate to, communicate with, and educate officers who either need daily help or more serious remediation for long-term lack of alignment with training. Supervisors may also need to acquire training in accessing and using an agency's accountability infrastructure, assuming that such infrastructure exists, when serious concerns and violations of officer activities occur. For example, supervisors need a clear understanding of the various internal discipline and internal affairs processes that help supervisors correct poor behavior, including how to use those processes. Supervisors may also need training on how body-worn cameras and automatic vehicle locators function with regard to their accountability effects. Again, everyday accountability mechanisms such as performance metrics, inspections, and audits are part of this accountability infrastructure that supervisors need training upon.

KNOWLEDGE FROM CRIMINOLOGY

It is the committee's evidence-informed judgment that major facts and theories from criminology, if integrated into police training curriculum, are likely to support the rule of law, protect the public, and prevent crime. Greater awareness of criminological theory and facts can help police in both the Global North and the Global South to understand the "where, why, how, who, and what" of crime problems and how interventions might disrupt the conditions or opportunities for crime. Incorrect beliefs or biases about who commits crime and where it is committed (and why) may lead to ineffective or even harmful policing tactics, including unnecessary use of force and arrest that neither protects the public nor supports the rule of law. This is the committee's collective opinion. As discussed later, evaluations of any police curricula, much less evaluations of instruction on crime fact and theory, are very limited. Little is known about the effectiveness of teaching specific content, either because such content has yet to be evaluated or evaluations focus on participants' perceptions of the curricula and short-term impacts and not on changes in behaviors or performance.

Nonetheless, the committee feels strongly that learning about research-supported facts and theories on crime and crime prevention can lead to the knowledge that better supports police participation in, and development of, evidence-based interventions. These facts include the "laws" of crime/problem concentration, the relationship between age and crime, and repeat victimization. Knowing about these concepts and facts may empower police organizations to better implement policies in ways that more effectively target resources while at the same time promoting the ROL and protecting human rights. Similarly, a grounding in basic criminology theory, especially deterrence and criminal opportunity theories, will support critical knowledge for policing.

It will be important to ensure that training at all ranks and units of the police organization draw from a shared conceptual model of crime, crime prevention, and policing interventions. Leaders particularly benefit from this knowledge by understanding how to allocate their scarce resources for crime prevention more strategically. Box 3-1 summarizes the key implications for practice from this section.

Key Facts and Concepts About Crime

One fundamental fact for police education at all levels is that criminal activity concentrates among a "power few" individuals (Sherman, 2007) and does so both geographically (Weisburd, 2015) and temporally. Eck and colleagues (2005) gathered together studies from 1970 to 2015 that provided quantitative data on crime distributions to produce a series of systematic reviews demonstrating the consistent and clear concentrations of crime across places (Lee et al., 2017), offenders (Martinez et al., 2017), and victims (O et al., 2017). The fact that crime concentrates is especially important knowledge for police leaders, who can design resource allocation strategies that balance emergency police responses and preventive approaches to building community safety. That balance, as substantial evidence shows (NASEM, 2018c; NRC, 2004), is more effective at reducing crime than reactive approaches that are less focused on specific places, times, and offenders. The following sections discuss how these laws of crime concentration could become the foundation for police curricula.

Concentration of Crime at Places

In 1989, Sherman, Gartin, and Buerger outlined the concept of a "criminology of place" when they discovered that three percent of micro places—which they called "hot spots"—produced 50 percent of all calls to police for service in Minneapolis, Minnesota. Weisburd, in his American Society of Criminology Sutherland Award address, emphasized that "the single most important empirical observation in the criminology of place is that crime concentrates at very small units of geography" (Weisburd, 2015, p. 135). The discovery of crime concentration is the foundation for crime prevention programs targeted at specific places, including hot spots policing (Weisburd, 2015). Lee and colleagues (2017), reporting on their systematic review, concluded that "there is no doubt that crime is concentrated at a small number of places regardless of how crime is measured, the geographic unit of analysis used, or type of crime" (Lee et al., 2017, p. 11). Their research is highly supportive of Sherman's (2007) "power few" argument and their findings support Weisburd's (2015) law of crime concentration in places. Two National Academies consensus committees (NASEM, 2018c; NRC, 2004) have also confirmed that policing interventions that focus on these crime concentrations can be effective in preventing and reducing crime at these locations.

> **BOX 3-1**
> **Key Implications for Practice:**
> **Knowledge Needed to Promote the Rule of Law**
> **and Protect the Population**
>
> The most useful knowledge with the strongest supporting evidence includes both facts and theories. Here are the key facts supported by cross-national evidence:
>
> - *Crime concentrates at specific and "micro" places:* Recognizing this criminological fact means that police can target (and conserve) resources better by focusing their problem-solving attention on specific micro locations that account for the most crimes and crime harm.
> - *Crime concentrates during specific times at these places:* Allocating police to the right places (hot spots) on the right days and times further sharpens police effectiveness at preventing crime.
> - *Crime concentrates among few offenders:* A large proportion of crime is committed by chronic offenders at specific places and times. These offenders engage in a wide range of offending behavior, with offenders who create the highest harm to the population in terms of severity or destructiveness often committing fewer crimes than the high-frequency offenders who contribute to less overall harm (i.e., minor offenses).
> - *Youthful offenders are likely to desist over time:* The vast majority of juveniles who commit minor offenses desist as they become adults. Police can safely divert from prosecution low-level offending by most young people, since most will stop offending regardless.
> - *Repeat victimization:* Repeat victimization is a pattern by which a small percentage of victims suffers a large percentage of all criminal victimization.
>
> Key theories that are supported by cross-national evidence are also relevant to effective policing:
>
> - *Routine Activities Theory:* Crime emerges when a likely offender converges with a suitable crime target in the absence of a capable guardian. Understanding people's everyday routines and the interaction between these routines and specific places can help officers understand *why* crime concentrates at certain places and times.
> - *Residual Deterrence Theory:* Short periods of police presence in a crime hot spot predict longer periods of no crime or disorder after police leave, not only at the immediate location of patrol but also in the surrounding vicinity.
> - *Displacement of Crime Falsified:* Many believe that if police target crime hot spots, crime will just move from one place to another. However, studies have not shown evidence for displacement. There can be a "diffusion of benefits," in that crime also goes down in areas around targeted hot spots.

Given these findings, the concentration of crime at specific places deserves a central place in police education. Not all neighborhoods are wholly "bad" or "good," but rather, specific places (street corners, particular houses or businesses, a specific location within a park, a portion of a long alleyway, etc.) have characteristics about them which are more likely to present opportunities for crime commission. Lee and colleagues (2017) explain that five percent of street segments account for around 42 percent of the crimes, whereas five percent of neighborhoods account for only around 20 percent of crimes. Recognizing this criminological fact means that police can target (and conserve) resources by focusing their problem-solving attention for the 20 percent *or less* of places that generate from 50 to 80 percent of all crimes and crime harm (Lee et al., 2017; Weinborn et al., 2017).

Understanding why criminal events occur at specific locations[2] (and how frequently) can provide insight into efforts to prevent such crimes from occurring. Eck and colleagues explain that "different types of crime have different spatial relationships, dependencies, structures, and distributions, which are the result of different social and spatial processes over an area" (2005, p. 67; see also Brantingham and Brantingham, 1993). That is, interactions at places vary because of the combination of routines, place features, and opportunity structures that make some places more prone to substantial crime concentrations.

The converse of the law of crime concentration is that there are large numbers of streets, homes, apartment blocks, and parks in even high-crime communities that are relatively crime-free (Sherman et al., 1989). Appreciating the routines, features, and opportunity structures in these crime-free "cool spots" can contribute to the knowledge and skills needed to apply strategies for maintaining cool spots or to cool down existing hot spots or build what is known as "collective efficacy" in local communities (Sampson et al., 1997). Recent evidence shows that the police can strengthen crime prevention in deprived communities, increasing the willingness of residents to take action and develop collaborative efforts to solve local problems (NASEM, 2018c; Weisburd et al., 2020).

Concentration of Crime Over Time

The law of crime concentration also applies to the temporal distribution of crime in high-crime places. Ratcliffe (2002) shows that the opportunities

---

[2]For example, this includes understanding why burglaries occur often in a specific part of a street segment, but not another; where vehicle thefts are most likely to occur; which stores, or bus routes, might be most prevalent for armed robberies; or which street corners attract violence or vice.

to commit crime are not evenly distributed spatially or temporally. From a resource deployment perspective, allocating police to the right places (hot spots) at the right times (hot times) is a fundamental leadership practice. It not only needs to be part of middle- and upper-level management education and training to improve police effectiveness and prevent crime; it also needs to be widely understood by patrol officers, who want to target hot spots at the right time and spend their job time in ways that align with the occurrence of crime problems.

Concentration of Most Offences Among Few Offenders

Research consistently shows that most individuals are law-abiding citizens who do not come in contact with the criminal justice system or else commit minor infractions infrequently. Only a small proportion of people commit a large proportion of crime (Blumstein et al., 1986; DeLisi, 2005; Hindelang et al., 1981; West and Farrington, 1977; Wolfgang et al., 1972). Put another way, a large proportion of crime is committed by chronic offenders who engage in a wide range of offending behavior (Kennedy, 1997). Police education therefore needs to balance the presentation of this research about the concentration of crime among a few offenders by emphasizing the law-abiding nature of most people.

Youth, Offending, and the Age-Crime Curve

An important key fact about crime and offenders is the "nonlinear relationship between age and crime" (Farrington, 1986, p. 236). Crime rates consistently increase from the minimum age of criminal responsibility (which can vary by country) to reach a peak in the teenage years. Farrington (1986) and many others have consistently argued that "the most plausible theory is that the age-crime curve reflects decreasing parental controls, a peaking of peer influence in the teenage years, and then increasing family and community controls with age" (Farrington, 1986, p. 236). Moffitt (2015) adds an important nuance to understanding juvenile offending. She differentiates between the vast majority of juvenile delinquents, who commit minor offenses and desist as they become adults, and the very small group of youth who will continue offending into adulthood.

The most critical implication of this pattern may be that police can safely divert from prosecution low-level offending by most young people, since most of these young offenders will stop offending regardless. Moffitt (2015) explains that most young offenders "age out" of offending, but there are a few young who are persistent/chronic offenders and engage in criminal behavior throughout the life-course. She further argues that the antisocial behavior of the latter life-course-persistent offenders tends to emerge in childhood. In contrast, offenders who age out of crime (adolescent-limited offenders) start to exhibit antisocial behavior around age 14 or 15, alongside puberty. Moffitt shows that "life-course persistent antisocial behavior emerges from early neurodevelopmental and family adversity risk factors, but adolescence-limited delinquency does not" (Moffitt, 2015, p. 593). She also notes that "life-course persistent antisocial development is almost exclusively male, whereas most female antisocial behavior is of the adolescence-limited type" (Moffitt, 2015, p. 593).

Repeat Victimization

Repeat victimization is a pattern by which a small percentage of the population suffers large percentages of all criminal victimization (Farrell, 1995). Such concentration on victims has been observed in repeat incidents of burglaries (Townsley et al., 2000) as well as in frequent reports among domestic violence and intimate-family-violence victims. Police who are taught to think very carefully about repeat victimization can aid in reducing crime by targeting support for certain individuals.

Relevant Theories in Criminology

Routine Activities Theory

One of the handful of criminological theories that should perhaps be considered for inclusion in the education curriculum at the police recruit level is routine activities theory. First articulated by Cohen and Felson (1979), the micro-level, place-based interpretation of this theory argues that crime emerges when a likely offender converges with a suitable crime target in the absence of a capable guardian. The everyday routines and social activities of people—going to work, attending school, socializing, and so on—contribute to these convergences at the particular places where people shop, eat, or socialize (etc.), such as certain street corners and bars, as Sherman and colleagues (1989) discuss. Understanding the public's routines and the interaction between these routines and specific places can help officers understand *why* crime concentrates at certain places.

Residual Deterrence Theory

According to general deterrence theory, crime rates in an area will reduce with continued police presence and the capacity to apprehend offenders. One of the big surprises to police officers in training is the deterrent effect of police patrols when police are not on the scene—and may not even have been there for days. The "residual" deterrent effect of police action was first observed by Sherman (1990) and tested by Koper (1995), who found that short periods of police presence in a crime hot spot (12–15 minutes) predicted longer periods of no crime or disorder after police left (up to 30 minutes). Ariel and colleagues (2020) confirmed this finding in an experiment on 115 London Underground platforms, in which patrol presence deterred crime up to the ticketing and street levels. Most surprisingly, Barnes and colleagues (2020) reported up to four days of residual deterrence in hot spots of 200 meters by 200 meters in an area in a Western Australia city, after a day with one patrol in each of those spots averaging about 15 minutes. Related findings were reported in two new experiments in the United Kingdom in 2021 (Basford et al., 2021; Bland et al., 2021). Hot spots studies have also used short dosages of police presence to successfully create a deterrent effect in crime hot spots (see, e.g., Kochel and Weisburd, 2019; Koper et al., 2021; Koper, Wu, and Lum, 2021; Rosenfeld et al., 2014; Telep et al., 2012; Williams and Coupe, 2017).

Displacement of Crime Proven False

A common misconception is that crime is simply pushed elsewhere when the police patrol high-crime places. However, after initial falsification of that theory by Weisburd and colleagues (2020), two systematic reviews have failed to find evidence in support of the displacement hypothesis (Bowers et al., 2011; Braga et al., 2019). Studies generally show that not only does hot spots policing *not* displace crime to places nearby, it may also cause a "diffusion of benefits." That is, that crime also goes down in the areas near the hot spots targeted for patrol.

Evidence-based Policing Approaches

In addition to learning about criminological theory, recipients of police training and education will likely benefit from learning about specific interventions shown to reduce crime by focusing on crime-prone places, people/groups at high risk of committing crime, and protection of victims. These approaches also have few adverse unintended consequences.[3] Much of this evidence has been reviewed in two National Academies consensus studies, *Fairness and Effectiveness in Policing* (NRC, 2004) and *Proactive Policing: Effects on Crime and Communities* (NASEM, 2018c).

---

[3] It is important to note that crime reduction alone does not justify a particular strategy. The costs associated with implementing some policing strategies, like Terry stops or the use of police officers in schools, can be large enough to outweigh any benefits associated with reducing the harm from crime.

High-risk Offenders: Focused Deterrence

To address high-risk offenders, police education could describe police tests of *focused deterrence* (Braga, 2008; Braga and Dusseault, 2018; Braga and Weisburd, 2015; Braga et al., 2019). Focused deterrence approaches (also known as "Operation Ceasefire" or "the pulling-levers approach") were reviewed in the National Academies' 2018 report on proactive policing. Such approaches have been used in the United States to reduce and prevent violence by high-risk offenders, gangs, and those involved in illegal drug markets. These programs reach out directly to individuals at high risk of committing serious violence in the future to communicate the threat of sanctions, the promise of surveillance, and the support of resources that can help integrate individuals back into law-abiding society and behavior. The strategy involves direct interaction with offenders and clear communication of incentives for compliance with the law in a procedurally just manner. The message is that not only must each individual not commit murder, but neither can any of their known associates. If someone in a rival group *is* murdered, the police and authorities will impose full enforcement on the entire social network suspected of causing the murder.

A meta-analysis of 24 focused deterrence strategy evaluations found moderate reduction in serious crimes (Braga et al., 2019). All but one of the studies[4] were conducted in the United States. Organizational structures and characteristics of street and organized crime gangs have been shown to differ considerably across cultures and regions (see Ratcliffe, 2016; Ratcliffe et al., 2014). The degree to which a focused deterrence strategy could achieve similar crime reduction outcomes in other parts of the world, particularly countries outside the Global North, is unknown. However, the difficulty in developing and testing such programs is not great. It could well be encouraged by donor nations, especially as an alternative to extra-judicial killing (which may be used in just such situations in many countries).

Low-level Offenders: Diversion

According to a systematic review of almost 30 experiments in Global North nations, police can prevent more crime and reduce harm by *not prosecuting* young first offenders who have committed relatively minor offences (Petrosino et al., 2010). Diversion makes good sense in most cases, because many young offenders desist from offending as they enter adulthood (see theories above). Police training could usefully include a module on diversion of young people (see Wilson et al., 2018) to build the skills necessary so that police optimize diversion opportunities to reduce repeat

---

[4] The exception was an evaluation conducted in Glasgow, Scotland.

youth offending. The application of diversion programs is similar for adult drug offenders (Hayhurst et al., 2019; Payne et al., 2008). The concepts of "net widening" (Decker, 1985) and "snares" in the criminal justice system need to be well understood by police. Police training on diversion (both adult and young people) should focus on the broader benefits of diversion to society as well as the individual offenders.

Domestic Violence Perpetrators: Targeting Offenders, Risk Assessment, and Protection Orders

As with crime in general, concerning domestic abuse it is a small number of (or "power few") domestic abusers who cause the most harm. Selective targeting of the most dangerous people could prevent many domestic murders and serious injuries; however, these people are often hard to identify, given that few domestic murders are preceded by any reports to police about violence in relationships. Training on these issues might encourage police leaders to launch digital records systems and collaborative relations with social agencies needed to identify the most dangerous domestic abusers.

Where information is available, threats or attempts of suicide by the future murderer may be the best way to predict homicidal behavior in a relationship. Neyroud's (2018) systematic narrative review of 31 studies explored the level of suicidal ideation within perpetrators of domestic homicide (as well as those of mass shootings and suicide terrorism). The review found that suicide ideation is three times more prevalent in domestic homicide perpetrators than in the general population. Previous suicide attempts are seven times higher in domestic violence perpetrators than in the general population. This work provides insights that might be instructive to police to help them be more targeted in their risk assessments of domestic violence and monitoring of protection orders.

Police training should be implemented so that police have the skills to administer validated risk assessments (Campbell et al., 2009; Roehl et al., 2005; Turner et al., 2019). Likewise, training should teach the skills needed to apply a screening set of questions when protection orders are processed to help police better monitor the "power few" (Sherman, 2007), who are most at risk for harming their partner or families.

While police training must be aligned with the laws of a jurisdiction pertaining to domestic and family violence, the training curriculum should be clear about the harm to victims, or even waste of resources, that can be caused through the mandatory arrest of offenders (Sherman and Harris, 2015; Sherman and Smith, 1992; Xie and Lynch, 2017). Police also may benefit from training in the law and application of protection orders, known variously as restraining orders, apprehended violence orders, and family violence orders. They may benefit as well in learning that, as Dowling and colleagues concluded, "protection orders are associated with a small but significant overall reduction in severe domestic violence re-victimisation … [yet they are less effective in cases of] less severe and non-physical forms of re-victimisation" (Dowling et al., 2018, p. 13).

High-risk Drug Offenders: Spatial Targeting

For high-frequency drug offenders, proactive arrests have a mixed impact on recidivism (Eggins, Hine et al., 2020), which suggests that police could likely increase public safety by limiting this type of tactic. By contrast, training officers to have the necessary skills to target, investigate, and conduct drug seizures could impact the collateral damage from drug dealing. With seizures targeting places at high risk of drug crimes (rather than people at high risk of committing drug crimes), it may be possible to reduce the harms of retail/street drug dealing. With the increase in drug availability in regional and rural areas (see Schalkoff et al., 2020), this type of spatial targeting of seizures to reduce harms to retail users could be explored as a part of police training.

High-risk Micro-geographic Places

Two National Academies reports (NASEM, 2018c; NRC, 2004) have come to fairly robust conclusions about place-based approaches in policing: when conducted legally and with an eye toward prevention rather than apprehension, they can effectively reduce and prevent crime in the short to medium term. By increasing officer presence at these places and adjusting or mitigating the environmental, social, and physical characteristics that contribute to crime concentration, crime can be prevented without the threat of displacement. As discussed earlier, effective place-based approaches specifically target micro-geographic locations, also known as hot spots, rather than the larger neighborhoods or communities that envelop them. Some notable hot spots include entertainment precincts (Eggins et al., 2020), road areas at high risk of accidents (Mazerolle, Eggins et al., 2019), places that attract mass gatherings and protests (Police Executive Research Forum, 2018), and some risky online communities (Davidson et al., 2020; Eggins et al., 2021).

At a minimum, effective place-based approaches involve increased police presence at micro hot spots to increase the perceived risk of apprehension by would-be offenders at those places. However, it is important to note that effective place-based approaches at micro-geographic hot spots mean more than simply having police presence at those spots. It is also not enough to place closed-circuit cameras or other technologies (license plate readers, gunshot detection systems, etc.) at those locations. Rather, what the police *do* at those hot spots is what matters immensely to their impact on crime (Lum and Nagin, 2017; Nagin et al., 2015). Studies reviewed by the National Academies (NASEM, 2018c) committee on proactive policing indicate that problem-solving and focused deterrence efforts related to crime hot spots can help to reduce crime. Community engagement in hot spots—while it alone may not necessarily reduce crime—could also improve citizen satisfaction and perceptions of the police and aid in problem-solving efforts. New research by Koper and colleagues (2021) has also found that hot spot approaches can produce large-scale, long-term crime reduction when practices are sustained and well managed.

It is also important to note that, as with all policing interventions, training on place-based interventions may be misinterpreted, creating harmful effects. For example, the concept of "hot spots" patrolling has been incorrectly interpreted by many police agencies in the Global North as aggressive crackdown approaches, which have employed unconstitutional or illegal uses of stop-and-search. In both the Global North and the Global South, targeting individuals has also resulted in excessive use of force, violations of human rights, and inequities in treatment across racial, ethnic, or religious groups. As aligned with the committee's broader goals of understanding what police strategies can simultaneously promote the rule of law and protect the public, training approaches for police have to strongly couple any training on prevention with training on protecting human rights and the dignity of people more generally.

CRITICAL POLICING SKILLS

This section describes key skills that police officers need to carry out evidence-based policing approaches. These approaches generally emphasize proactive policing, as opposed to reactive approaches, as core to preventing crime. Proactive strategies necessitate greater problem-solving and critical thinking to address crime problems and increase the frequency of interactions with the public. Abilities such as building multi-agency partnerships, communications skills, and interviewing are also needed within police organizations.

Critical Thinking Skills

As outlined above, to absorb a large portion of the scientific knowledge related to effective policing requires critical thinking, not just rote memory. Successful implementation of tactics, operations, strategies, and activities beyond routine technical processes requires complex analysis not often associated with policing. To promote the rule of law and protect the public, police officers will benefit from acquiring more knowledge and skills in how to *think*—and not just how to march, write reports, physically detain someone, or use their vehicles or weapons. Many of the policing approaches discussed above and in the committee's first report (NASEM, 2021) use problem-oriented policing, proactivity and crime analysis, community- and citizen-centric approaches, or geographic targeting that require critical and creative thinking skills.

Critical thinking skills include an array of dispositions and have been defined by several groups and scholars. The *Delphi Report* on critical thinking (Facione, 1990) brought together several international experts who concluded that an ideal critical thinker would be

> habitually inquisitive, well-informed, trustful of reason, open-minded, flexible, fair-minded in evaluation, honest in facing personal biases, prudent in making judgments, willing to reconsider, clear about issues, orderly in complex matters, diligent in seeking relevant information, reasonable in the selection of criteria, focused in inquiry, and persistent in seeking results which are as precise as the subject and the circumstances of inquiry permit (p. 2).

The translation of these concepts to an evidence-based policing approach is straightforward. Scholars have argued that critical thinking is essential and closely coupled to evidence-based practices in other front-line fields, such as nursing (see, for example, Finn, 2011; Profetto-McGrath, 1999, 2005; and Staib, 2003).

For example, as described in this committee's first report (NASEM, 2021), problem-oriented policing is an evidence-based approach that begins with a fundamental assumption: no event, call for police service, or public safety incident is unique or unrelated to other events (Goldstein, 1979, 1990). Instead, events are connected by some underlying problem or causal mechanism. Thus, problem-oriented policing requires an officer to discern where *and* why crime clusters by using data to examine possible reasons why crime repeatedly occurs in a particular location or why a group or individual repeatedly commits crime in certain ways. Proactive problem-solving to prevent future crimes may also require officers to engage with various members of the public, including groups with whom an officer may not be accustomed to collaborating.

Thus, problem-solving requires officers to be inquisitive, apply analytical and theoretical knowledge, make well-informed judgments that are contextualized to the environment and community, and rationalize, judge, and weigh the costs and benefits of their actions. Critical thinking in problem-solving also means that an officer can take theoretical or evaluation knowledge about crime or police interventions, synthesize various pieces of knowledge, and then apply that knowledge to physical actions.

The Scanning, Analysis, Response, and Assessment model of problem-solving (Eck and Spelman, 1987) includes an evaluative and assessment component, which requires building on existing knowledge by assessing current actions. In sum, many aspects of a problem-solving approach require critical thinking skills.

Data Skills

As noted above, a problem-solving approach requires officers to make decisions based on data and, more importantly, on data that are appropriately collected, collated, and analyzed as to be accurate. Police agencies must have systems that can reliably produce information about crime and police interactions. Such systems will include an accountability infrastructure to monitor and audit the collection and reporting of data. Accurate counts of crime and measurement of trends in crime as well as outcomes of police interventions are essential for tracking and maintaining police effectiveness.

Examples of useful measurements include crime-mapping of high-frequency and high-harm "hot spots," rank-ordering of the most frequently or seriously harmed repeat victims, rank-ordering of people returning from prison to local communities by their prior or predicted seriousness of offending, forecasting the highest-risk places and people likely to suffer high harm from violence or other crime, counting indicators of internal challenges such as officer absenteeism and public complaints, and tracking the before-and-after differences in the effects of police policy changes.

Frontline officers will need the skills to report data accurately and be able to understand basic crime trends and outputs of the type of measurements identified above. Such skills include the ability to make sense of basic graphs and plots and to understand implications of structural biases in the data (e.g., presented data on crime reported may not reflect crime incidence). It is also important to ensure a grounding in basic statistical concepts that are linked to their operational and reporting requirements; such concepts may be appreciating the uncertainty in statistical analyses and understanding the difference between data analysed to show current trends and data analysed for forecasting purposes. Supervisors will need the skills to be able to monitor whether data are recorded accurately and to determine trends accurately to direct operations and officer assignments. Management, for appropriate policy development and response, will need the skills to understand trends over time and the significance of results from tracking the before-and-after differences in the effects of police policy changes. Higher-level data skills will also be useful for understanding any misinterpretations of the trends and the complexities of cause, effect, and magnitude of effect.

Interacting with the Public

Police officers routinely interact with the public. These interactions require that officers treat people professionally, respectfully, and lawfully, regardless of whether they have committed a minor offense, a serious crime, or no crime at all. One way to do this is to develop officers' *cultural humility* and awareness of their own implicit and explicit biases. Cultural humility is defined by flexibility, a lifelong approach to learning about diversity, and a recognition of the role of individual bias and systemic power in interactions (Agner, 2020). Cultural humility is considered a self-evaluating process that recognizes the self within the context of culture (Campinha-Bacote, 2018). Such practices have been effectively implemented in other public service-oriented fields, such as health care and education (NASEM, 2020), and could be expected in policing.

Implicit biases are expected to play a role in differential treatment by police with diverse populations. Interventions designed to address these biases may assist in motivating improvements to police behaviors to create more fair and just interactions with all members of the public. However, current evaluations of implicit-bias training indicate that it cannot stand alone but should be integrated with broader departmental policy strategy (Kahn and Martin, 2020). Meta-analyses demonstrate small positive effects of implicit bias interventions but only for a short period (Forscher et al., 2019). A systematic review of interventions designed to reduce implicit bias found that many such interventions are ineffective, and some may even increase implicit biases (FitzGerald et al., 2019).

Improved interactions between police officers and the public could also benefit from a training curriculum on police legitimacy and procedural justice. Studies have shown that when police practice procedural justice, citizen satisfaction with the police improves, among other benefits. Procedural justice training for police recruits has also resulted in higher ratings of desired on-the-job behaviors by mentors (Antrobus et al., 2019). In addition, training that aims to guide officer thought processes and slow down reactions through supervisory intervention has been shown to reduce officer use of force and potentially unjustified or unnecessary discretionary arrests (Owens et al., 2018). Procedural justice training for officers conducting random roadside breath testing found that people stopped by trained officers were more likely to report changing their views on drinking and driving, as well as to report higher levels of satisfaction and compliance (Mazerolle et al., 2012).

At the committee's workshop, an example of implementing a three-day procedural justice training in Mexico City was highlighted (Canales, 2021). The training was organized into four key elements: (1) describing police legitimacy/trust as the principle of operational efficacy; (2) outlining the four principles of procedural justice and associated tools, mindsets, and tactics to integrate them into policing; (3) discussing the structural complexities of the citizen-police relationship; and (4) reviewing Mexico City's policing history. A survey of trainees[5] showed moderate to large effects of the training on how police officers thought about procedural justice, distributed across each of the four principles. Additionally, because of the training, those police officers in the treatment group became more identified with the profession of policing and the institution of the Mexico City Police and their perception of citizens improved through the training. Trained police officers also improved their behaviors in the field relative to control officers, as demonstrated through a "mystery shopper" evaluation instrument. For police officers whose managers had also been trained, the effect size of the training on the frontline officers was 30 percent larger. This moderator effect highlighted the importance of linking training to broader organizational factors. Following the study, the Mexico City Police opted to train all their officers in procedural justice and weave the training into the recruit academy and the police university, emphasizing organizational justice.

Relatedly, regarding interactions with the public, police training on de-escalation and use of force has received much recent attention. The committee will examine policies and practices to reduce officer use of force and effective training methods on this topic in its third report.

Communicating, Collaborating, and Building Multiagency Partnerships

The facts and theories about crime and crime prevention discussed above can be drawn on to help police understand why working cooperatively with other service providers, such as child social services, educational services, healthcare workers, and therapists, can in some cases prevent crime more effectively than prosecution and imprisonment. For example, Mazerolle and colleagues (2019) found that programs where police are trained to work in partnership with schools to implement family treatment

---

[5]The research team took a baseline survey of where the officers stood on ideas of procedural justice, and then evaluated the officers four to six months following the training through different instruments to measure each of the three trust factors. A second measure of whether officers internalized their training was drawn from photo journaling and interviews. These data showed officers shifting from an identity of being a strong enforcer of the law to being a trusted protector of the population, helping citizens feel safe. The third and most powerful measure was on observer coding of police officer behavior in simulated interactions. The coding measured whether trained officers changed their behaviors if they had received training. Across three perceptions of the assigned evaluation, coders found similar effects—both in size and direction—to those they found in the surveys. The survey responses were consistent with the coded behavioral impacts of the training on how police officers addressed interactions in the field.

groups in combination with case management show some promise. These programs benefit both the students and the families that are involved (Mazerolle et al., 2019). They may be beneficial to include as a central part of police training to address youth crime issues.

Police would need to develop the skills necessary to work with local and government partners in providing integrated services to the different types of adults and youth with whom they come into contact. Good communication skills and the ability to work cooperatively with other people and entities will necessarily be important. Another skill that cuts across many aspects of efforts to protect victims is interviewing. Some of these skills are taught in existing training modules, such as procedural justice training and specialist hostage negotiation training. However, police organizations would likely be well served if they made learning these skills foundational at all levels of police training.

Powell (2013) offers a range of insights into police interview training, concluding that "good questioning comes from specialised training programs incorporating ongoing spaced practice exercises, exemplars of best practice, expert instruction and feedback" (p. 713). These skills are central for police to develop because research finds that effective interviewing of victims can "increase the volume of information a complainant provides and has the potential to increase the credibility of this evidence" (Bull, 2014, p. 1). This is particularly the case for sexual assault victims (Westera et al., 2019).

Many of the evidence-based policing approaches discussed above require a relationship between police and other agencies and entities. For example, to support diversion and focused deterrence, officers would need to know about and have access to child and adult social services to follow through with these tactics. When targeting places at high risk of crime, a central aspect of police work is partnering with other agencies and community members to regulate, control, and prevent crime (Mazerolle and Ransley, 2006). Police likely benefit from training in ways that foster good working relationships with property owners, building inspectors, environmental regulators, education department representatives, community groups, insurance companies, business leaders, and local government personnel.

The police are likely to encounter a myriad of issues and to come into contact with delinquent youth and their families, child and elderly victims, people with mental illness (Kane et al., 2018; Livingston, 2016), people with disabilities (Morgan, 2021; Wright, 2018), domestic violence perpetrators and victims,[6] and members of organized crime

---

[6]Globally almost one in three women have experienced intimate partner violence, non-partner sexual violence, or both once in their lifetime. See https://www.unwomen.org/en/what-we-do/ending-violence-against-women/facts-and-figures.

groups,[7] among others. A common theme in research and practice is the need for police to work as a partner in multi-agency response to these encounters. For example, Eggins and colleagues (2020) in their rapid review of criminal justice responses to child abuse found that "collaboration between child victim advocates, law enforcement and multi-disciplinary teams in child sexual abuse investigations may benefit case outcomes by increasing the satisfaction in non-offending caregivers of victims and the likelihood of successfully prosecuting child sex offenders" (p. 28).

Breckenridge and colleagues (2016) evaluated integrated responses to domestic violence,[8] identifying some common benefits such as "a broader range of services that are offered beyond the initial crisis period, improvement of the professional knowledge base and service provider relationships, facilitation of responsive and prompt decision-making, increased cross-program or agency collaboration on case management, and provision of multiple entry points for clients to access support" (2016, p. 3).

A review by Mazerolle and colleagues (2021) of efforts to target organized crime groups found that it is important for police to take time to build trust and shared goals among partners, not overburden staff with administrative tasks, build in targeted and strong privacy provisions for intelligence sharing, and provide access to ongoing support and training for multi-agency partners. As such, programs and training curricula could be formed for select officers to develop specialized skills and techniques for setting up and running multiagency partnerships and building the capacities to understand and structure privacy provisions around sharing intelligence data.

Likewise, multiagency cooperation and joint training are important in relation to crowd control. The Police Executive Research Forum (2018) report suggests that police "training together can help agencies achieve a coordinated response with all agencies in agreement about tactics and rules of engagement. Interagency training can also serve as a training of trainers and allow agencies with advanced skills (in areas such as mobile field force) to share their knowledge" (p. 34).

CONCLUSION

This chapter has drawn on the scientific literature and the strongest findings about crime and crime prevention to identify knowledge and skills useful for police to promote the rule of law and protect the public. It

---

[7]Such as in groups for drug distribution, human trafficking, money laundering, terrorism, gun markets, and child exploitation.

[8]In protecting victims of domestic violence, a partnership-building organization includes the Multi-Agency Risk Assessment Conferences (MARACs) that aims to reduce harm to high-risk domestic violence victims. Representatives from various agencies contribute information during the MARACs, producing a positive, measurable impact in victims' lives (Robinson, 2006).

organizes knowledge around the key facts about crime, significant criminology theories, and evidence-based policing approaches. It identifies skills necessary for proactive evidence-based policing, including critical thinking, interacting with the public, and collaborating and building multiagency partnerships. The committee believes that if police understand the evidence about what works (and what does not) and have a sound understanding of criminological theory and the mechanisms that cause crime problems, then they may have a better chance of using their police powers in ways that are fair and effective.

The capacity to train officers on the scientific evidence base for policing requires more than just convincing officers of the merits of basing their actions and decisions on a reliable body of scientific knowledge. Receptivity to this knowledge is low, and such knowledge is generally considered by officers to be inferior to both experience and anecdotes (see Lum et al., 2012; Telep and Lum, 2014; Telep, 2016b). Such research knowledge needs to be translated into digestible forms that officers can easily understand, including the stories of research projects and successes in crime prevention, so they can institutionalize that knowledge into actual police tactics, operations, strategies, and technologies (Lum and Koper, 2017).

It is important to note that very few training programs, in the Global North or the Global South, have been subject to rigorous evaluation that uses officer behavior in the field as an outcome.

If policing is to become a global profession that values evidence as a foundation and uses evidence to guide police policy and training, it must develop the capacity to collect and analyze data necessary to regularly refresh curricula and to ensure that police educators and trainers are equipped with the latest information about crime and effective solutions. What might be the foundations for education and training now might change or be refined over time.

4

Training Methods and Delivery

While the previous chapter examined the knowledge and skills needed for police to promote the rule of law (ROL) and protect the population, in this chapter we address the second part of our task by answering the question, *What is known about mechanisms (e.g., basic and continuing education or other capacity building programs) for developing the core skills needed for police to promote the ROL and protect the population?* The committee sought to find answers to the "how to teach" questions that should be considered when developing police training. One of the papers commissioned by the committee for this report (Herold, 2021) demonstrated that little robust evidence is available on the effectiveness of different methods of police training in any context, let alone evidence on how effectiveness of the same methods might vary in different countries with different levels of prior education and experience.

The committee recognizes that there is additional need for more research and knowledge on the effectiveness of different police training methods. This need is just as important as the need to understand the effects on officer behavior of specific knowledge imparted by training (see Chapter 3), since what is taught and how it is taught are intricately linked.

This chapter examines both the training environment and instructors and draws attention to current challenges that exist with common forms of police training. It briefly summarizes learning theories and best practices for training design. It also identifies five studies that compared different methods of police training across varying contexts and countries. Our central conclusion is that the way police officers are trained likely matters as much as the skills and knowledge on which they are trained.

Yet the evidence for what might constitute effective training methods remains limited. In order to build a more robust evidence base and inform future training efforts, training approaches that donor agencies like the U.S. Department of State, Bureau of International Narcotics and Law Enforcement Affairs support should be tracked and evaluated with regard to implementation and effectiveness in achieving specific outcomes (such as protecting the population and supporting human rights and the ROL).

SETTINGS FOR POLICE TRAINING

An international review of police recruit training programs reveals that 17 of the 24 programs studied separated training into two primary settings and separate "standalone blocks"—residential/academy and field training (Belur et al., 2020). Police recruits in U.S. municipal police departments, for example, receive an average of approximately six months of basic academy training and approximately four months of field officer training (Reaves, 2016). In less common instances, field training may be followed by a final block of learning within an academy setting (Belur et al., 2020). Officers in other parts of the world (e.g., Estonia, Croatia, and Germany) often receive longer periods of basic training or, as in Finland and Norway, are required to attend three-year police universities (Council on Criminal Justice Task Force on Policing, 2021a). There is also a variation in who pays for the training: in the U.S. setting, it is common for police agencies to cover a recruited officers' pay and training costs, and in other countries the officer may be responsible for this. Depending on the institutional constraints on how much officers can be paid, and the nature of the supply and demand for police officer positions, differences in the incidence of the cost of training could affect how much training officers receive. The frequency and dosages of additional in-service and specialized training not only vary but, for some, neither is available at all. In some agencies or nations, specialized training may only be available to a privileged few.

Recruits tend to first learn within an academy, which provides a controlled learning setting that involves classroom instruction. Classroom instruction can vary widely; some agencies use only lecture-based instruction, while others may use role-playing and mock situations.

Academy training is typically followed by experiential learning within a field-training setting, often without a return to the classroom. These two basic settings are most likely to be sequential, not alternating or combined. The symbolic overtones of those locations and their separation are substantial, especially given the usual sequence of classroom training followed by in-the-field training. This sequence gives rise to the widespread cliché allegedly voiced by the field training officers (FTOs): "Forget what they told you in the academy; we'll show you how police work is really done," thus creating a "stigma" against content taught in the recruit academy (Hundersmarck, 2009). The sequential separation of training, moving from the classroom to the streets, appears to leave recruits particularly vulnerable to the predilections, and possible failings, of either their academy instructors or their FTOs. Sequencing academy training to be followed by experiential or field training—without some reinforcement between the two—may undermine or allow recruits to disregard knowledge learned in one setting and not the other.

In addition, police might receive in-service training after they are fully certified or serving as full-time police officers. In-service training can take place in a variety of settings, including informally during an officer's shift by a supervisor requesting adjustments to an officer's behavior, or during daily roll calls to update officers on new policies, laws, or equipment (see a creative approach to roll call training in Box 4-1). In addition, in-service training could involve officers returning to an academy setting for a few hours or days to obtain certain certifications, such as in firearms use or in responding to specific situations, or else to acquire specialized new knowledge (Martin, 2020), such as in evidence-based policing, procedural justice, de-escalation training, or learning about a new reporting or analytic system. A variety of teaching methods have been used across these various needs for in-service training (e.g., lecture/classroom-based, web-based, simulations, role-play scenarios, supervisory meetings).

Finally, police officers and other police supervisors and commanders may attend specialized in-service training programs that are not offered to everyone, such as INL's International Law Enforcement Academies training or other seminars or training offered by external organizations, non-governmental organizations, or other nations.

PROBLEM-SOLVING TECHNIQUES

Transferring the core knowledge and skills outlined in Chapter 3 will require training methods that activate critical thinking, problem-solving, communication and conflict resolution, and community organization skills (Birzer and Tannehill, 2001; Bradford and Pynes, 1999). While the evidence is mixed concerning recruit and trainer perceptions of the effectiveness of problem-based learning, at least one study found that those exposed to problem-based learning techniques acquired thought processes that better supported and aligned with community policing strategies than those trained using traditional style methods (see McGinley et al., 2019).

Some recruit training has adopted problem-based learning strategies, including scenario-based training, in efforts to develop higher-level problem-solving and decision-making skills (see Werth, 2011). One quasi-experimental study reported that police recruit academy trainees

> **BOX 4-1**
> **Micro-Training (Workshop Presentation)**
>
> During the public workshop on May 27, 2021, Eric Beinhart of the International Criminal Investigative Training Assistance Program (ICITAP) at the U.S. Department of Justice presented on the utility of micro-training as an international police training technique. ICITAP uses the terms "roll call" and "micro-training" (MT) interchangeably. The Los Angeles Police Department first implemented MT in 1948 after it found that first-line supervisors had about 20 minutes of their allotted time remaining after calling the shift roll calls in which daily orders or other pertinent information for the shift was provided to officers. First-line supervisors could present MT modules during these periods on law enforcement topics including: defensive tactics, proper arrest techniques, how to protect a crime scene, how to hold a community meeting, interviewing techniques, and proper use of force, to name but a handful of countless possible topics. MT is not informal training because it should utilize formal lesson plans like regular training. MT offers a holistic approach to skill-based learning and education when it is used to complement and reinforce a traditional training infrastructure. Beinhart offered five key advantages to using MT, including: (1) the ability to train police in their own stations, (2) the broad range of potential topics that can be taught, (3) the ability to disseminate standard operating procedures rapidly, (4) because MT modules are short, the flexibility to present in local languages, and (5) the potential to add many hours of training over the course of the year, without ever requiring officer absences from their worksites.
>
> Beinhart highlighted four specific MT techniques: (1) role-plays (ideal for capturing and sustaining the attention of those involved and the audience), (2) photographic posters (versatile approach for when trainees may have poor literacy rates or speak different languages), (3) the instructor asking trainees questions to keep them involved in the learning process, and (4) classic didactic lectures.
>
> ICITAP partnered with the Sierra Leone Police in a U.S. Agency for International Development (USAID)-funded program to develop nine modules of MT to

believed problem-based learning produced better problem-solving and critical thinking skills than lecture-based academy training (Vander Kooi and Palmer, 2014). The integration of other learning theories, including cognitive load theory (stressing knowledge retention and skills acquisition), have been suggested (Mugford et al., 2013). The degree to which these types of integration have occurred in police academies is currently unknown.

Relatedly, training methods also need to take into account the abilities of trainees. For instance, in countries where basic literacy levels may be low, a combination of written, pictorial, and verbal dissemination of knowledge is likely required to share news or policies in ways that are accessible to all officers. Similarly, as Eric Beinart noted in a presentation to help mitigate violence before, during, and after the presidential, parliamentary, local council, and mayoral elections in 2012. The MT modules focused on improving police relationships with citizens and civil society, particularly with disenfranchised youth. The modules were designed in English with 10 master instructors as part of an instructor development course taught by Beinhart (phase one). The 10 master instructors then trained 733 more police instructors in the nine modules as well as more than 120 civil society leaders, including priests, imams, paramount chiefs, members of community policing boards, and the media (phase two). Then these instructors trained police at the station level and local civil society leaders in a variety of tribal languages, such as Mende, Temne, Mandinka, and Fula. This dual pronged approach of MT teaches police what they should be doing, while simultaneously teaching citizens what police should be doing—thus improving the chances that citizens will hold police accountable for their actions. Anecdotally, the Sierra Leone MT was viewed as a success, as election observers reported high levels of professionalism among police officers, neutrality at the polls, and very few complaints logged against police following the election. USAID commissioned an evaluation of this program (Davis et al., 2012).

Beinhart explained that if a police department presents 20 minutes of MT three times a week, this will add up to a total of 52 training hours over the course of a year. MT allows officers to continuously train and stay up to date on relevant information at their police stations, without incurring the logistical expenses of traveling to training sites. ICITAP advocates designing and implementing pilot MT projects in different countries around the world that incorporate good project design (including baseline data), monitoring, and evaluation. These projects would emphasize outcomes and outcome measures to measure progress in achieving project objectives.

NOTE: This speaker summary is presented as a factual accounting of what was presented at the workshop for the committee's consideration. The statements reflected here are those of the individual presenter and do not necessarily represent the views of all workshop participants or the committee.

the committee, where access to reliable Internet or cell service is challenging, the use of radio for training can provide more reliable communication to support consistent training goals. While radio is not a secured means of relaying information, it is valuable for reaching a large number of people across a wide area. Where Internet or WiFi is more reliable, social media groups and apps may also present opportunities for training that can be disseminated through a messenger platform. However, social media groups can often be peer-based with little senior management participation and little to no oversight, which can make sharing (and fact-checking) information through typical face-to-face training processes more challenging. See Box 4-2 for further discussion about the importance of adapting training to local realities.

> **BOX 4-2**
> **Importance of Adapting Training to Local Realities (Workshop Presentation)**
>
> Tom Parker, United Nations Office on Drugs and Crime, shared his experiences with policing working in the Balkans, Iraq, and Nigeria over the past several years. His first takeaway was the importance of using local solutions to solve local problems. For example, he highlighted the tendency of using retired police officers, often from the Western world, to train law enforcement overseas. But unless those trainers have a considerable amount of experience in their new environment, he discouraged this as a strategy; because their home-country experience will be vastly different from that of the group they are brought in to train and generally will not be applicable to the context in which they currently find themselves. Instead, Parker suggested finding people from peer institutions or countries to conduct trainings, while still keeping in mind political and competitive concerns between countries within a region.
>
> When designing trainings, Parker emphasized the importance of obtaining a granular understanding of the needs of local stakeholders. He shared an example of working with fingerprint experts in a country without realizing that even though every state police office had a fingerprint section, none of them was capable of lifting a fingerprint from a crime scene because their equipment was broken and the forensics units did not go to crime scenes directly. Parker advocated for those overseeing or designing trainings to go out into the field, go on patrol with police units, and visit various units and laboratories to get a better sense of the realities and needs of that particular police force.
>
> Parker further highlighted the importance of aligning training appropriately to resources available within a country. For example, training police to collect evidence to Western standards with regards to contamination and chain of custody in an environment where there is nowhere to store it and where it cannot be forensically analyzed is a pointless endeavor. He added that not every solution needs to be high-tech, especially in locations where electrical power is unreliable. For example, he explained that the Central Criminal Records Office in Lagos, Nigeria, has a double-index-card analog system. Currently, fulfilling a records check request can take three months. Although digitizing Nigeria's archive may be attractive, Parker pointed out that most police stations in the country will not have computer access to a centralized network for a number of years. Instead, he suggested providing a phone number and personnel to answer calls so that anyone could call the office for access to needed records.
>
> NOTE: This speaker summary is presented as a factual accounting of what was presented at the workshop for the committee's consideration. The statements reflected here are those of the individual presenter and do not necessarily represent the views of all workshop participants or the committee.

INSTRUCTORS

Box 4-3 provides an example of a local training that had global impact—where people with related experience from a peer country were employed as peer trainers to conduct trainings. It is not known how frequently this is done and whether other outcomes are as successful as in this example. The present state of research fails to provide a comprehensive picture of the characteristics of police personnel providing police training instruction. Even less information is available about the skills of people typically tasked with designing training curriculum content and selecting training methods. Much more information and knowledge is needed about not only who is training police officers, but also who is best suited to carry out this vital task and with what training background.

The trustworthiness of agency leadership and instructors appears to influence training outcomes (MacQueen and Bradford, 2017). Instructors with a particular prior police experience, or with certain dispositions,

---

BOX 4-3
Illustrative Example: Cross-National Peer-to-Peer Training

During the committee's public workshop, discussion arose about training at the local level that bridged impacts at the international level. For example, field investigators and prosecutors who participated in successful war crimes investigations in Sarajevo and Srebrenica in the 1990s were used as peer trainers in Sudan. In 2004, in co-ordination with the International Criminal Court and the U.S. State Department, their trainees conducted a large-scale survey among more than 1,000 refugees who had fled genocide in Darfur. The cross-national peer-to-peer training provided by investigators and prosecutors was effective in transmitting essential skills for evidence collection. The lawyers and investigators involved posed direct and specifically designed questions to sampled respondents who had experienced violence: questions addressed whether the assailants were dressed in official government uniforms, the numbers of victims involved in the violence, the nature of their wounds (what kinds and how many), and whether these injuries were observed directly, among other details. The results of the survey were presented by the United States to the United Nations Security Council and the Senate Foreign Relations Committee and played a major role in the indictment of Sudanese President Omar al Bashir (Hagan et al., 2006). In this way, peer trainers skilled in transmitting techniques for legally relevant evidence contributed to essential knowledge of levels and kinds of rule-of-law violations, which are essential to form incident estimates and to address evidentiary questions raised in important international legal proceedings. Such effective cross-national peer-to-peer training to enhance the rule of law and protect the public through prosecution and field investigation could be an informative model for police capacity-building efforts.

may not be the best trainers for all training purposes. A tendency to select instructors with certain characteristics may lead to the underutilization of highly effective female, younger, or minority officers. Instructors with a penchant for sharing their experiences (e.g., "war stories") in an attempt to engage officers may actually create barriers to the effective delivery of a problem-solving training curriculum (see Chappell and Lanza-Kaduce, 2010). Further, such training methods have been argued to misrepresent actual police working conditions and duties (Belur et al., 2020), further reinforcing distorted perceptions concerning the dangers or mandates of police work and shifting focus away from problem-solving or community-centric policing. Moreover, as Grace Longe, Assistant Commissioner of Police of the Nigerian Police Force stated: some commanders may send officers to act as trainers as a punishment or a demotion, negatively impacting how the training is viewed by the trainer, the trainee, and the larger organization.

FTOs are thought to play a critical role in socializing officers by demonstrating and reinforcing police agency and community values outside of the academy setting. This socialization process may influence field application of academy training, trainee behaviors, and any misconduct. For example, research demonstrates a significant correlation between the misconduct of FTOs (Getty et al., 2016), peers (Ouellet et al., 2019), and officers. Research also finds that some FTOs actively negate academy learning (Hundersmarck, 2009). Thus, field training assignment—particularly to FTOs who engage in/fail to address officer misconduct as well as assignment to FTOs who do not provide training congruent with academy curriculum—could harm police training outcomes.

The persistent fear that FTOs may not be advancing the ROL or the protection of the public was highlighted by the murder of George Floyd by Dereck Chauvin, a Minneapolis Police Department officer, in 2020. On the day Chauvin killed Floyd, he was serving as an FTO and training two other officers, despite the fact that he had been the subject of several prior complaints, including three shooting incidents.[1] Those two recruits were then charged under state law with aiding and abetting second-degree murder and second-degree manslaughter, as well as under federal law against deprivation of civil rights.[2] Floyd's murder reflects the worst-case scenario of an FTO selection process failing to screen out unsuitable instructors. More generally, instructors both for the police academy and field training should be equally qualified, armed with not only the same

---

[1] See https://edition.cnn.com/2020/06/05/us/minneapolis-officers-background-george-floyd-trnd/index.html, downloaded August 10, 2021.

[2] https://www.reuters.com/world/us/after-chauvin-sentencing-charges-remain-police-officers-floyd-case-2021-06-25/, downloaded August 10, 2021.

knowledge and skills to promote the ROL, as well as to protect the population, alongside the ability and moral code to convey, teach, and inculcate this knowledge in others.

The committee found no studies documenting the qualification process or disciplinary records for FTOs in any nation. Nor did it find any studies of the possible differences in training outcomes across FTOs with and without records of disciplinary violations, such as studies examining whether there may be higher levels of recruit misconduct among officers trained by FTOs who themselves had substantial evidence of misconduct. (However, see Getty et al., 2016, which found concentrations of complaints against recruits with a small portion of FTOs in Dallas, Texas). Given the major role that FTOs play in so much training of the police, the lack of attention to the selection and management of the FTO training work is a serious global gap in police knowledge.

Furthermore, instructors' cultural competency may also impact police training outcomes. To accurately assess situational threats, officers must be able to address personal biases and be able to communicate despite potential religious, ideological, cultural, and identity barriers (Gerspacher et al., 2019). To the extent that instructors are unfamiliar with these barriers within a particular jurisdiction (e.g., U.S. officers training lacking cultural competency within an international context), they may be ill equipped to serve as effective instructors.

TRAINING DESIGN

Many of the most effective forms of professional development have a basis in theories of adult learning (Institute of Medicine, 2010; Salas et al., 2012). Several disciplines—such as adult education, cognitive science, developmental psychology, industrial and organizational psychology, neuroscience, and sociology—have advanced theories of learning and knowledge translation as well as developed science-informed steps for the design and evaluation of training. The perspectives on learning are complex; with adult learning seen as dependent on sociocultural contexts (NASEM 2018a,b). The question of the effectiveness of training design rests on what is attained in knowledge, skills, attitude, and improved job performance as a result of training.

A number of best practice principles are available through the work of both researchers and industries. A fundamental principle is that effective training is developed through a systematic process (Brown and Sitzmann, 2011; Goldstein, 1986, 1991; Salas et al., 2012). Such a process includes conducting a training needs analysis, developing training objectives, selecting training methods, pilot testing the training design, and evaluating the outcomes of training. These fundamental steps of training design apply to all levels of trainees, from entry-level to management, as well as to instructors themselves in cases where training is aimed at preparing future instructors.

A training needs analysis should include assessments of the physical and cognitive tasks of individuals and teams, drawing on critical incident analyses for tasks with variable approaches. The needs analysis should also include an investigation of the organizational climate and state of the workforce (Harvey, 1991). It is important for training designers to take into account the conditions that might affect training delivery and outcomes, such as whether the organization is ready to support the training and to make use of the knowledge and skills from the training. Research has shown that features of the organizational environment—such as how supportive managers and coworkers are toward integrating new knowledge and skills—influence the application of training to the job (Blume et al., 2010; Ottoson and Patterson, 2000; Rouiller and Goldstein, 1993).

An understanding of the workforce capacities will help determine which training methods and resources best fit the training situation. A best practice for delivery is to use methods and tools that make the training as similar as possible to the tasks on the job (Brown and Sitzmann, 2011; Schmidt and Bjork, 1992). Training designers will also have to consider methods most likely to engage target learners in ways that they comprehend and that best allow them to retain knowledge and skills from the training (Noe, 2010; Salas et al., 2012). For high-risk, high-stake situations, hands-on experiential training can raise the psychological fidelity of the experience over classroom training by providing environmental conditions with simulated difficulties, time pressures, and other aspects similar to the actual situation. Personnel are able to practice managing their emotions while learning to handle high-risk job events (National Research Council, 2013).

Durable, long-term learning is best accomplished by repeated experience with critical tasks and skills. Research supports target learning distributed over multiple training sessions instead of relying on one-time training programs. Single, shorter trainings tend to result in short-term performance that predictably deteriorates over time (Cepeda et al., 2006; Rawson and Dunlosky, 2011; Soderstrom and Bjork, 2015). Additionally, trainings that are interconnected with links to shared knowledge and skills can strengthen long-term memory of key information and functions (NASEM 2018a,b).

In general, people make decisions in two ways. One way is more systematic and analytic and relies heavily on working memory. The other relies more on affective and emotional processes (Kahneman, 2003; Sloman, 1996; Stanovich and West, 2000). In nonstressful situations, working memory works in concert with emotional processing. In stressful situations, one's capacity to draw on working memory can be compromised, leaving emotional processing to influence decisions (Beilock, 2008, 2010;

Wang et al., 2005). Further, time pressures may limit one's ability to take in new and important information and make reasoned decisions. Optimal decision-making in stressful situations requires an awareness that emotion-driven decisions occur, and when they are most likely to occur, as well as the appropriate mental models to react quickly. Research has shown that simply making people aware of common internal responses in stressful situations (e.g., sweaty palms, beating heart) can make these responses less distracting (Jameison et al., 2010). Training can be directed at normalizing such physiological responses to lessen the impact on effective reasoning (Mattaralla-Micke et al., 2011). Training can employ realistic, stressful situations and explore the consequences (both positive and negative) of all possible decisions. Such education could also address cultural norms that might drive decisions that are inherently risky and driven by emotions.

One study of learning outcomes at police training academies (Vodde 2009, 2012) illustrated the usefulness of applying insights from adult learning theories to police training. This work emphasized six best practices:

1. Explain why the information contained within curriculum is critical knowledge needed to perform their duties;
2. Align content with previous knowledge and competencies to increase openness to new concepts and combat mental rigidity;
3. Promote methods that include self-directed learning and autonomy;
4. Create environments and systems that support and reinforce a continuous learning culture;
5. Use application-focused exercises to demonstrate the content's usefulness to solve current problems; and
6. Instill self-determination to learn.

As noted previously, rigorous research on the effectiveness on specific police trainings is largely absent. Much of what is known about training design comes from other work contexts, particularly from health care and medical settings (Institute of Medicine, 2010; Wheller and Morris, 2010). Recent randomized trials, however, have started to examine changes to officer behavior after procedural justice training (Owens et al., 2018; Wheller et al., 2013). One study (Owens et al., 2018) found that officers who participated in the training were less likely to resolve incidents with an arrest and to be involved in incidents where force was used than officers who did not participate in the training. Both studies provide encouraging signs of effectiveness of training in altering officer behavior on the job (NASEM, 2018c).

Training should have clear, specific goals and the training should be piloted and/or evaluated to verify how close the training came to meeting these goals. A strong evaluation moves beyond counting participants and participants' reactions to training but is results oriented—the participants' knowledge, competence, and performance are assessed (e.g., do the participants transfer what they learned to the job?) (Moore et al., 2009). Further, an evaluation may assess the extent to which police interactions with citizens improve or community perspectives of police improve as a result of training and changes in training participants' behaviors.

EVALUATIONS OF TRAINING METHODS

While a growing number of police trainings are subjected to scientific inquiry, the review of the literature in one of the commissioned papers (Herold, 2021) found that most evaluations of training assess training impact in relation to trainees' attitudes on the training, a few test policing outcomes post training, and even fewer test the effectiveness of methods on learning. Moreover, the evaluations identified in this review were all conducted in the Global North. A prior systematic review of all recruit training evaluation studies (McGinley et al., 2019) found that more than half (61%) have been conducted in the United States, followed by Australia (14%), the United Kingdom (9%), and Canada (8%). It is suspected that the geographic concentration of police training studies limits the generalizability of existing knowledge to places with different political structures, economies, and cultures.

Most of the rigorous police training evaluations have focused on procedural justice training (see, for example, Antrobus et al., 2019; Mazerolle et al., 2012; Murphy et al., 2014; Owens et al., 2018; Rosenbaum and Lawrence, 2017; Sahin et al., 2017; Wheller et al., 2013). Other rigorous police training evaluations have examined implicit bias training (Worden et al., 2020), de-escalation training (Engel et al., 2020), social interaction training (Aremu, 2006; McLean et al., 2020), training to reduce police use of force and improve decision-making (Andersen and Gustafsberg, 2016), officer resilience training (Chitra and Karunanidhi, 2021; McCraty and Atkinson, 2012), and training to improve attitudes toward workplace diversity (Platz et al., 2017).

In general, these studies suggest that training can change targeted police behaviors, justice-related outcomes, and police-public interactions (see references in Chapter 3). However, not all evaluations of police training report positive impacts on all expected outcomes (see La Vigne et al., 2019, for an example of disparate training outcomes across six U.S. cities). The committee thinks more evaluations are needed to identify how and why some police training practices are more effective than others and in what contexts. Further experimentation is needed to accurately attribute programs' successes or failures to curricula, methods, and/or organizational contexts.

The Herold paper (2021) identified five studies that examined the outcomes of unique police training methods, each systematically comparing a single teaching method with other methods designed to teach the same content. The five studies were conducted in four different Global North countries. Each study focused on a different training topic and assessed a different teaching strategy. Two evaluations were conducted using randomized controlled trials; three were conducted using quasi-experimental designs. Four of the five training method evaluations found evidence of improved learning or performance outcomes in one method compared to the alternative. Given the small number evaluations, the committee is not able to draw strong conclusions about which methods are most effective for particular training topics. We share the description of these studies to illustrate how one might investigate the effectiveness of different approaches to police training. (See also Box 4-4 for ideas for implementing tracking and evaluation of police training.)

BOX 4-4
Tracking and Evaluating Training Outcomes
(Ideas from Workshop Discussion)

- Supplement input metrics (e.g., number of officers trained) with development of meaningful outcome metrics (e.g., measures of officer or instructor performance pre/post training).
- Conduct short-term and longer-term surveys of officers/trainees to determine if they remember training, use any of the material or techniques, and/or if the training changed their attitude about policing.
- Conduct rigorous evaluations of repeated trainings to ensure their efficacy and role in the daily work of officers.
- Develop and maintain databases of training and officers trained. May be necessary to develop policies and infrastructure so that training data can be shared effectively across departments and users.
- Collaborate with other federal agencies on monitoring and evaluating impacts of training.
- Create partnerships with local universities to help track impacts of police training.
- Record case studies of donor investments in training and relevant impacts in precincts (e.g., lowered homicide rate). While success stories can generate interest in continued gathering of data, documenting failures can help identify contextual and organizational barriers to return on investments.

Study #1: Training in Ways to Interview Sexual Assault Victims, U.S.

Lonsway (1996) conducted a quasi-experimental study comparing three different ways of teaching police officers how to interview sexual assault victims. The training was conducted in the basic academy offered by the University of Illinois, Police Training Institute for newly appointed municipal officers from across the state. One class of 56 officers was given the traditional sexual assault response police academy training (with one hour devoted to the topic). Two other classes of 56 officers each received different experimental training protocols. One experimental protocol (E1) delivered to a recruit class a nonstop, stand-alone *sexual assault simulated victim interview workshop* of 3.5 hours' length, which included 30 minutes of lecture. The other experimental group's protocol (E2) featured an integrated curriculum interspersing three sessions among other classroom topics, for a total over multiple days of 4 hours of sexual assault response training, comprising 90 minutes of lecture and interactive discussion, 60 minutes of simulated role-play and discussion, with 90 minutes of lecture, discussion, and a videotaped interview of a rape victim.

While all three groups exhibited similar knowledge at entry, after participating in the workshops the group members in condition E1 were more likely to address victim welfare, suspect responsibility, and broader police investigatory options. E2 participants demonstrated greater proficiency in interviewing content and style. The authors concluded that E1 (a single intensive and focused workshop), rather than E2 or the traditional training, was the best of the three approaches. The author suggested that a single intense session would be best to improve learning for specialized topics that recruits cannot yet connect to a broader understanding of police functions.

Study #2: Basic Police Recruit Training at Academies, U.S.

Vodde (2009) conducted a quasi-experimental study comparing learning outcomes among recruits between two New Jersey basic police training academies. The first academy generally used traditional militaristic pedagogic-style instruction. The second academy used teaching methods aligned with best andragogical principles intended to facilitate adult learning (Vodde, 2009). The academy using best andragogical principles was found to produce better outcomes. In addition to greater learner satisfaction, problem-based learning assessments revealed that recruits in the andragogical-centered academy showed greater critical thinking, communication, problem-solving, and decision-making competencies than recruits who received traditional academy training methods.

Study #3: Procedural Justice Training, England

Wheller and colleagues (2013) used a randomized controlled trial to evaluate the Greater Manchester Police's procedural justice training in England. A traditional classroom-based teaching method was compared to two combinations of classroom-based and scenario-based teaching methods. The authors found no statistically significant differences in outcomes across delivery methods but argued that the size of their participant pools might have hindered meaningful training group comparisons.

Study #4: Training in Taking Child Witness Statements, U.K.

Adams and colleagues (2019) conducted a randomized controlled trial to assess a Child Interview Simulator game, which was codesigned with U.K. police forces. The game was designed to help police recruits learn to take initial child witness statements. Assessment outcomes found that recruits who participated in the game learning displayed better tacit understanding, including demonstrations of empathy and attention, compared to those who received the same curriculum in face-to-face training. The recruits taking the face-to-face instruction displayed lower levels of understanding about the importance of gaining child respect through tactics used in the interviewing process.

Study #5: Training in Self-defense Against Knife-wielding Persons, Germany

Koerner and colleagues (2020) used a mixed-method quasi-experimental design to assess differences between two methods for teaching defense techniques against knife-wielding persons to 20 German police recruits. In what the study called "linear" training, learners were taught by a trainer how to execute knife movements and other techniques. In what was called "nonlinear" training, learners were taught by scenario-based, problem-solving discussions that focused on how to execute decisions. The authors report that, while both groups improved their performance in a nine-week post-training retention assessment, those receiving the nonlinear teaching method showed greater increases in problem-solving abilities than those receiving the linear training. In simulated knife attacks, the nonlinear training group were struck less and ended attacks faster and more frequently than the linear training group participants.

Nonetheless, qualitative evaluation found that the nonlinear group was less satisfied with their training, desiring more technique-focused rather than decision-making instruction. Thus, in addition to providing evidence of what the best knife attack training for police is, this experiment further suggests that learner evaluations of teaching quality may be wildly different from important outcomes of the training. For policing in particular, this study emphasizes the importance of tracking behavioral outcomes, and not just choosing teaching methods based on their popularity with students.

CONCLUSION

Despite some attempts to evaluate police training programs, almost nothing is known about the effects of how training is delivered in the policing context. More scientific work is needed to understand which training methods can best help police to acquire the knowledge and skills necessary to promote the ROL and protect the population. While this is true for both the Global North and the Global South, for the purpose of this report, the opportunity to continue research may be greater in the Global South.

While the policing landscape has shifted substantially over the past two decades (see Cordner and Shain, 2011), much recruit training worldwide is still delivered through traditional militaristic-style instruction. Field-training methods also have characteristics that may undo lessons learned in academy training. In-service training may reinforce old traditions, cultures, and practices that work against sought-after reforms or modernization goals for policing. Few studies have focused on assessing the independent impact of teaching methods, but available evidence suggests that teaching methods selected for curriculum delivery can directly affect officer learning. Importantly, a training instructor's characteristics and competencies may influence officer learning receptivity and performance outcomes.

Evaluations of training with methods based on best practices for adult learning in other professions are both relevant and encouraging. They suggest that adult learning models may be appropriate to develop the types of knowledge and skills officers need to more effectively promote the rule of law and protect the population. As discussed in Chapter 3, modern police work likely requires skill-building in areas that extend far beyond the basic task-oriented curriculum that has historically dominated police training. Research directly testing the impact of revised training methods is needed to determine if they could improve on traditional lectures, or even on "war story" discussions that use many anecdotes but fail to provide systematic knowledge (Sherman et al., 1998). Ideas for necessary evaluations and future research are discussed further in the next chapter.

5

Committee Conclusions

The committee was asked to consider the core knowledge and skills needed for police to promote the rule of law and protect the population and examine the state of evidence on the best mechanisms for acquiring that knowledge and those skills. In undertaking this study, the committee drew on information gathered from two commissioned papers (Herold, 2021; Mazerolle, 2021), a public workshop on police training in the global context, and our collective knowledge.

As discussed in Chapter 2, training is more likely to be successful if it is part of an overall strategy to reform police actions and if steps are taken to remove impediments for applying knowledge and skills from training to police practice (see Box 5-1). Foreign assistance donors should consider the main objectives of specific reform efforts and the steps required to achieve the reform, including the need for new units or leaders, incentive structures, new technologies, partnerships with local community groups, and political support. After essential strategies are determined, the types of training needed to support the reform efforts should be considered.

> **CONCLUSION 1:** Training needs to be launched in concordance with other organizational systems to reinforce its message, so that it becomes part of a comprehensive policing transformation, including changes to incentive, accountability, supervisory, and deployment structures that support training goals.

In conducting its review and determinations of training needs, the committee sought a new vision for policing, one in which police have learned to

> **BOX 5-1**
> **Assessment of Cultural Factors**
>
> Political, economic, social, cultural, organizational, and individual barriers to the implementation of police training vary across contexts. For example, police agencies looking to adopt training that has proven effective elsewhere might face legal (e.g., limits on police authority) or financial (e.g., lack of funding) obstacles unique to their own national or local governing structures and resources. Moreover, it is important to understand the context-specific forces that drive crime and violence in specific regions or countries and adapt training to be relevant to those factors (Ratcliffe, 2015). Cultural differences in societal expectations, perceptions of police, and differences in local customs and norms can be expected to affect how a specific form of police training will impact officers and communities. Agency structures and resources and officer education levels or prior training experiences can also can play a role in whether replication of training is successful across contexts. At a minimum, global efforts to advance security and justice reform through police training require government and police buy-in, separation of the police from military forces, police accountability systems, the public's belief that police can protect them, police partnerships with human rights organizations, and intimate knowledge of local institutional and societal conditions (see Bayley, 2001).
>
> SOURCE: Herold, 2021.

think critically about preventing crime as opposed to strictly responding to crime and hunting criminals. A focus on crime prevention requires developing cognitive and decision-making capacity. The committee supports an evidence-based approach to policing where police and management use scientifically derived information to strengthen decision-making and policing tactics and strategies.

The committee reached a consensus on five connected principles of police training that are grounded in an evidence-based approach and that can support the rule of law and the protection of the public. These principles are laid out in Chapter 1 and expanded upon in subsequent chapters. First, training must do no harm. Second, police training must provide *specific* knowledge and skills to promote the rule of law and protect the population effectively (as discussed in Chapter 3). Third, police training should use effective teaching methods and practices (as discussed in Chapter 4). Fourth, policing training should be continually evaluated to ensure that it produces the desired police practices and behaviors. Fifth, the delivery of training needs to be flexible and contextualized, given the resources, cultures, and capacities of different police agencies that the U.S. Department of State, Bureau of International Narcotics and Law Enforcement Affairs supports.

CONCLUSION 2: An evidence-based approach to police training emphasizes five principles: that training should do no harm; that training activities, tactics, and strategies should be supported by good evidence; that the educational training methods used are also effective; that organizations continuously track, test, and evaluate training efforts; and that the delivery of training needs to be flexible and contextualized.

In the committee's experience, police generally lack a conceptual framework for understanding the root causes of crime and decision-making, which can impede their ability to protect the population and uphold the rule of law. Greater awareness of criminological theory can help police to understand the causation of crime problems and provide insight into how interventions might disrupt the conditions that create opportunities for crime. The committee believes that if police understand the evidence about what works (as well as what does not), and if they have a sound understanding of criminological theory alongside the mechanisms that cause crime problems then they may have a better chance of using their police powers in ways that are fair and effective. For at least five decades and across the world, criminological research has shown that crime in cities is highly concentrated in certain micro-geographic places with certain people committing most reported crimes, which are committed against some victims far more often than other victims. The fact that crime concentrates is especially important knowledge for police leadership, which can design resource allocation strategies that strike a balance between emergency police responses and preventive approaches to build community safety (see Chapter 3).

CONCLUSION 3: Training on the causes and patterns of crime (and antisocial behavior), rule of law, and human rights is needed in both recruit training and advanced training of police. Such training includes a foundation of criminological theories and empirical facts that develop an understanding of how and why crime concentrates among certain offenders, places, times, and victims.

Key facts about crime derived from scientific research include the following:

- *Crime concentrates in a small fraction of all places:* Recognizing this criminological fact means that police can target (and conserve) resources better by focusing their problem-solving attention on places that account for the most crimes and crime harm.
- *Crime concentrates at certain times of the day and days of the week:* Allocating police to the right places (hot spots) at the right times (hot times) and on the right days (hot days) improves police effectiveness at preventing crime.

- *Crime concentrates among few offenders:* A large proportion of crime is committed by a small proportion of all offenders who chronically display a wide range of offending behavior, with offenders who create the highest harm often committing fewer crimes than the high-frequency offenders who contribute to less overall harm.
- *Youthful offenders are likely to desist over time:* The vast majority of juveniles who commit minor offenses desist as they become adults. Police can safely divert from prosecution low-level offending by most young people, since most will stop offending regardless.
- *Crime concentrates among repeat victims:* Repeat victimization is a pattern by which a small percentage of victims suffers a large percentage of all criminal victimization, and an even greater proportion of all crime harm.

Criminological theories also help police to understand the mechanisms that create crime problems. They offer insight into how interventions might disrupt the conditions that create crime opportunities and can support an officer's more critical and problem-solving approach to dealing with crime problems. Four key theories of crime causation that are supported by extensive multinational research have substantial relevance to policing:

1. *Routine Activities Theory:* Crime emerges when a likely offender converges with a suitable crime target in the absence of a capable guardian. Understanding people's everyday routines and the interaction between these routines and the opportunities for crime at specific places can help officers understand *why* crime concentrates at certain places and times.
2. *General Deterrence Theory:* Crime is reduced in populations that see continuing evidence of police presence and capacity to apprehend offenders; crime rises sharply when that capacity is sharply reduced (for example, in police strikes or when police ignore crime-prone places).
3. *Residual Deterrence Theory:* Short periods of police presence in crime hot spots applied in intermittent and unpredictable ways can lead to longer periods without crime or disorder after police leave, not only at the immediate location of patrol but also in the surrounding vicinity.
4. *No Evidence of Immediate Spatial Displacement:* Police agencies often argue that by targeting particular places, times, and people within those place and times, that crime will simply "move around the corner" and be displaced. Robust evidence indicates that displacement is not common, and that surrounding areas are more likely to see a diffusion of benefits, when police target specific crime hot spots.

In addition to a knowledge about crime, offending, and victimization, training must also include the extensive knowledge now available from evaluation research in criminology on protecting the public, effective crime preventative approaches, harm reduction, or improving the ability of the police to support the rule of law (for extensive reviews, see NASEM, 2018c and NRC, 2004). There is scientific consensus on several policing approaches that they can be appropriately adjusted to varying policing contexts to reduce crime and improve police-citizen relationships. These findings suggest that the following are effective approaches (see Chapter 3):

- Targeting of high-risk micro-geographic places or "hot spots" of crime, especially using problem-solving approaches;
- Focused deterrence strategies for high-risk offenders;
- Diversion for low-risk and youthful offenders;
- Risk assessment and protection orders to protect domestic violence victims from further abuse; and
- Spatial targeting of high-risk drug offenders within the drug market environment.

CONCLUSION 4: Officers must be trained on tactics, strategies, and actions that have been shown through high-quality research to effectively promote the rule of law and protect the public.

Science-based training on the causes and patterns of crime as well as on effective crime prevention approaches can complement ethics-based training on the rule of law and human rights. Training that links both helps to achieve Principle 1, that training should do no harm.

CONCLUSION 5: Training on the consequences of violating the rule of law and human rights principles can help police understand the role they play within society and the degradation that may occur to their authority when they abuse their power or fail to control police torture and corruption.

In carrying out evidence-based approaches, police would generally emphasize proactivity as core to preventing crime, as opposed to reactive approaches. Proactive approaches necessitate greater problem-solving and critical thinking to address crime problems and tend to increase the frequency of interactions with the public. Problem-solving aimed at crime prevention requires public participation. Abilities such as building multi-agency partnerships, communications skills, and interviewing are also needed to direct offenders and victims to appropriate resources as well as to gather information from the community to address crime hot spots.

A problem-solving approach requires officers to make decisions based on data and, more importantly, on data that are appropriately collected, collated, and analyzed as to be accurate. Frontline officers will need the skills to report data accurately and be able to understand basic crime trends and analyses. Supervisors will need the skills to be able to monitor that data are recorded accurately and to determine trends accurately to direct operations and officer assignments. Management, for appropriate policy development and response, will need the skills to understand trends over time and the significance of results from tracking the before-and-after differences in the effects of police policy changes.

CONCLUSION 6: Training is essential on skills for interacting with the public, and for problem-solving with partnerships for proactive responses guided by critical thinking and data analysis. Police training that includes content and analysis of routine data collection is likely to help police better identify and prioritize high-risk people, places, and vulnerable victims.

Although training methods may be an integral part of the outcomes of any training content, there is ample reason to believe that training methods themselves require a separate body of evidence. The world of adult learning has become increasingly innovative in the 21st century, with online learning rising rapidly in its use and efficiency. At the same time, interactive methods have become better understood and more acceptable to learners. Approaches to police training have ranged in form, including not only classroom-based lectures and scenario and field training, but also online modules with virtual simulations and also role-play with members of the community.

Police trainings have engaged both fellow police and outside experts as instructors. The characteristics and competencies of training instructors likely influence officers' learning receptivity and performance outcomes (see Chapter 4). The committee noted from some experiences that receptivity to training can be improved by immersing trainers in local contexts or using local trainers, as well as by designing training in line with local needs and alongside local stakeholders. Further, the dosage (time spent on training and any re-training) has varied by content and context (including variations in the available resources). Assessing these methods of instruction is just as important as examining the effects of content in an effort to better understand which approach works best for what purpose and in which contexts.

While rigorous evaluations of police training are becoming more commonplace, the committee was not able to draw strong conclusions about which methods are most effective for particular training topics given the few existing evaluations of comparing methods for police training.

Many of the most popular and frequently used police training programs remain unevaluated. Recent examples include de-escalation training (Engel et al., 2020) and implicit bias training (Council on Criminal Justice Task Force on Policing, 2021b; Spencer et al., 2016), both of which have been widely adopted following demands by community leaders and residents, despite lacking strong evaluation evidence that the training will change officer behaviors and lead to the outcomes sought. Rigorous evaluations of police training require multiple assessments, examining whether participants have understood and remember the training, whether they have internalized the material in ways that reflect how they think about themselves as police officers and their duties, and whether the training had an effect on skill development or changed behavior (e.g., do police effectively use the tactics, resources or knowledge from training and have they been implemented regularly in practice?).

Additionally, in line with Principle 1 that training should do no harm, evaluations of police training should examine the potential of harmful effects on both the community and police themselves (Anderson and Burris, 2017; Sparrow, 2008). Well-intentioned policing for crime reduction can result in unwanted community consequences that ultimately outweigh any benefits (see Tankebe, 2020, for an example of counter-terrorism policing interventions that likely encourage radicalization). Assessments of police training should take a holistic view of the impact of police training and ensure that training evaluations test for unwanted and potentially negative effects on the community and officers themselves.

While many training assessments often test participants' recall and understanding, the absence of rigorous evaluation on the impacts of training on actual officer behaviors in the field leaves critical questions unanswered. Ideally, rigorous evaluations of police training outcomes occur before widespread promotion and implementation of specific training programs; however, it is possible to conduct an evaluation in concert with implementation, learn from assessments, and make improvements to training.

CONCLUSION 7: Given the lack of research on teaching effectiveness in the policing context, implementation of promising methods should be evaluated to confirm whether they support officer learning and use of knowledge and skills in practice. Finding effective ways to train police officers, with knowledgeable and respected instructors, using experiential and problem-oriented approaches is key to advancing reform-based training from an evidence-based policing perspective.

Such research can be supported locally. Supporting locally appropriate research and development of content can take many forms, including consultations with major institutions (national, regional, or local) about the content, context, goals, and sustainability of each training program. Moreover, foreign assistance donors might be well positioned to foster collaboration and partnerships between universities and police academies to promote ongoing collaboration and sharing of lessons learned and good practice across institutions.

References

Adams, A., Hart, J., Iacovides, I., Beavers, S., Oliveira, M., and Magroudi, M. (2019). Co-created evaluation: Identifying how games support police learning. *International Journal of Human Computer Studies, 132*, 34–44.

Agner, J. (2020). Moving from cultural competence to cultural humility in occupational therapy: A paradigm shift. *American Journal of Occupational Therapy, 74*(4).

Andersen, J.P., and Gustafsberg, H. (2016). A training method to improve police use of force decision making: A randomized controlled trial. *SAGE Open, 6*(2).

Anderson, E., and Burris, S. (2017). Policing and public health: Not quite the right analogy. *Policing and Society, 27*(3), 300–313.

Antrobus, E., Thompson, I., and Ariel, B. (2019). Procedural justice training for police recruits: Results of a randomized controlled trial. *Journal of Experimental Criminology, 15*(1), 29–53.

Aremu, A.O. (2006). The effect of two psychological intervention programmes on the improvement of interpersonal relationships of police officers in Osogbo, Nigeria. *Criminal Justice Studies, 19*(2), 139–152.

Ariel, B., Sherman, L.W., and Newton, M. (2020). Testing hot-spots police patrols against no-treatment controls: Temporal and spatial deterrence effects in the London underground experiment. *Criminology, 58*(1), 101–128.

Barnes, G.C., Williams, S., Sherman, L.W., Parmar, J., House, P., and Brown, S.A. (2020). *Sweet spots of residual deterrence: A randomized crossover experiment in minimalist police patrol.* https://osf.io/preprints/socarxiv/kwf98/.

Basford, L., Sims, C., Agar, I., and Harinam, V. (2021). Effects of one-a-day foot patrols on hot spots of serious violence and crime harm: A randomized crossover trial. *Cambridge Journal of Evidence-Based Policing, 5*(4).

Bayley, D.H. (2001). *Democratizing the Police Abroad: What to Do and How to Do It.* Washington, DC: US Department of Justice, Office of Justice Programs. https://www.ojp.gov/pdffiles1/nij/188742.pdf.

Beilock, S.L. (2008). Math performance in stressful situations. *Current Directions in Psychological Science, 17*(5), 339–343.

Beilock, S.L. (2010). *Choke: What the Secrets of the Brain Reveal About Getting It Right When You Have To.* New York: Simon & Schuster, Free Press.

Bella, T., Bellware, K., and Kornfield, M. (2021). Chauvin failed to follow training, used 'excessive' force during Floyd arrest, experts testify. *The Washington Post.* https://www.washingtonpost.com/nation/2021/04/06/live-updates-chauvin-trial-resumes-after-police-chief-condemns-officer-absolutely-violating-policy-while-restraining-floyd/.

Belur, J., Agnew-Pauley, W., McGinley, B., and Tompson, L. (2020). A systematic review of police recruit training programmes. *Policing: A Journal of Policy and Practice,* 14(1), 76–90.

Bingham, T. (2011). *The Rule of Law.* Penguin Books.

Birzer, M.L., and Tannehill, R. (2001). A more effective training approach for contemporary policing. *Police Quarterly,* 4(2), 233–252.

Bland, M.P., Leggetter, M., Cestaro, R., and Sebire, J. (2021). Fifteen minutes per day keeps the violence away: A crossover randomized controlled trial on the impact of foot patrols on serious violence in large hot spot areas. *Cambridge Journal of Evidence-Based Policing,* 5(3).

Blume, B.D., Ford, J.K., Baldwin, T.T., and Huang, J.L. (2010). Transfer of training: A meta-analytic review. *Journal of Management,* 36(4), 1065–1105. doi.org/10.1177/0149206309352880.

Blumstein, A., Cohen, J., Roth, J.A., and Visher, C.A. (Eds.). (1986). *Criminal Careers and "Career Criminals."* Washington, DC: National Academy Press.

Bottoms, A.E., and Tankebe, J. (2017). *Police Legitimacy and the Authority of the State.* Hart Publishing Limited.

Bowers, K., Johnson, S., Guerette, R.T., Summers, L. and Poynton, S. (2011), Spatial Displacement and Diffusion of Benefits Among Geographically Focused Policing Initiatives. *Campbell Systematic Reviews,* 7, 1–144. https://doi.org/10.4073/csr.2011.3.

Bradford, D., and Pynes, J.E. (1999). Police academy training: Why hasn't it kept up with practice? *Police Quarterly,* 2(3), 283–301.

Braga, A.A. (2008). Pulling levers focused deterrence strategies and the prevention of gun homicide. *Journal of Criminal Justice,* 36(4), 332–343.

Braga, A.A., and Dusseault, D. (2018). Can homicide detectives improve homicide clearance rates? *Crime & Delinquency,* 64(3), 283–315.

Braga, A.A., Turchan, B., Papachristos, A.V., and Hureau, D.M. (2019). Hot spots policing of small geographic areas effects on crime. *Campbell Systematic Reviews,* 15(3), e1046.

Braga, A.A., Weisburd, D., and Turchan, B. (2018). Focused deterrence strategies and crime control: An updated systematic review and meta-analysis of the empirical evidence. *Criminology and Public Policy,* 17(1), 205–250.

Brantingham, P.L., and Brantingham, P.J. (1993). Environment, routine and situation: Toward a pattern theory of crime. *Advances in Criminological Theory,* 5, 259–294.

Breckenridge, J., Rees, S., Valentine, K., and Murray, S. (2016). Meta-evaluation of existing interagency partnerships, collaboration, coordination and/or integrated interventions and service responses to violence against women: Key findings and future directions. *Sydney: ANROWS.*

Brown, K.G., and Sitzmann, T. (2011). Training and employee development for improved performance. *APA Handbook of Industrial and Organizational Psychology,* 2. Washington, DC: American Psychological Association.

Bull, R. (Ed.). (2014). *Investigative Interviewing.* Springer Science & Business Media.

Campbell, J., Webster, D., and Glass, N. (2008). The danger assessment: Validation of a lethality risk assessment instrument for intimate partner femicide. *Journal of Interpersonal Violence,* 24(4). https://www.dangerassessment.org/uploads/DA_Validation_of_a_Lethality_Risk_Assessment_Instrument-Campbell.pdf.

REFERENCES

Campinha-Bacote, J. (2018). Cultural competemility: A paradigm shift in the cultural competence versus cultural humility debate – Part I. *The Online Journal of Issues in Nursing, 24*(1). https://ojin.nursingworld.org/MainMenuCategories/ANAMarketplace/ANAPeriodicals/OJIN/TableofContents/Vol-24-2019/No1-Jan-2019/Articles-Previous-Topics/Cultural-Competemility-A-Paradigm-Shift.html.

Canales, R. (2021). *The Effects of Procedural Justice Training for Police Officers in Mexico City*. Innovations for Poverty Action. https://www.poverty-action.org/study/effects-procedural-justice-training-police-officers-mexico-city.

Cepeda, N.J., Pashler, H., Vul, E., Wixted, J.T., and Rohrer, D. (2006). Distributed practice in verbal recall tasks: A review and quantitative synthesis. *Psychological Bulletin, 132*, 354–380.

Chappell, A.T., and Lanza-Kaduce, L. (2010). Police academy socialization: Understanding the lessons learned in a paramilitary-bureaucratic organization. *Journal of Contemporary Ethnography, 39*(2), 187–214.

Cheung, A.Y. (2019). *Measuring the Measures: Rule of Law Indices and Abusive Legalism*. https://doi.org/10.31228/osf.io/8r5zb.

Chitra, T., and Karunanidhi, S. (2021). The impact of resilience training on occupational stress, resilience, job satisfaction, and psychological well-being of female police officers. *Journal of Police and Criminal Psychology, 36*(1), 8–23.

Cohen, L.E., and Felson, M. (1979). Social change and crime rate trends: A routine activity approach. *American Sociological Review, 44*(4), 588–608.

Cordner, G., and Shain, C. (2011). The changing landscape of police education and training. *Police Practice and Research, 12*(4), 281–285.

Council on Criminal Justice Task Force on Policing. (2021a). *Effectiveness of Police Training*. https://counciloncj.foleon.com/policing/assessing-the-evidence/iv-effectiveness-of-police-training/.

Council on Criminal Justice Task Force on Policing. (2021b). *Implicit Bias Training*. https://counciloncj.foleon.com/policing/assessing-the-evidence/vii-implicit-bias/.

Davidson, J., Schimmenti, A., Caretti, V., Puccia, A., Corbari, E., Bogaerts, S., Schilder, J.D., Scally, M., Bifulco, A., and DeMarco, J.N. (2020). Exploring policing and industry practice in the prevention of online child sexual abuse. *Child Sexual Abuse*, 657–677. Academic Press.

Davis, A., Etter, L., and Fiorello, M. (2012). *Microtraining and the Sierra Leone Police: An Evaluation of the Effectiveness of Cascade Training*. Washington, DC: US Agency for International Development. https://pdf.usaid.gov/pdf_docs/pdacx405.pdf.

Davis, D. (2006). Undermining the rule of law: Democratization and the dark side of police reform in Mexico. *Latin American Politics and Society, 48*(1), 55–86.

Decker, S.H. (1985). A systematic analysis of diversion: Net widening and beyond. *Journal of Criminal Justice, 13*(3), 207–216.

DeLisi, M. (2005). *Career Criminals in Society*. Sage Publications.

Dowling, C., Morgan, A., Hulme, S., Manning, M., and Wong, G. (2018). Protection orders for domestic violence: A systematic review. *Trends & Issues in Crime and Criminal Justice*, (551), 1–19.

Eaton, K. (2008). Federalism, parties, and civil society in Argentina's public security crisis. *Latin American Research Review, 43*(3), 5–32.

Eck, J., Chainey, S., Cameron, J., and Wilson, R. (2005). *Mapping crime: Understanding hotspots*. Washington, DC: US Department of Justice, Office of Justice Programs. https://www.ojp.gov/ncjrs/virtual-library/abstracts/mapping-crime-understanding-hot-spots.

Eck, J.E., and Spelman, W. (1987). *Problem-Solving: Problem-Oriented Policing in Newport News*. Washington, DC: Police Executive Research Forum.

Eggins, E., Hine, L., Higginson, A., and Mazerolle, L. (2020). The impact of arrest and seizure on drug crime and harms: A systematic review. *Trends and Issues in Crime and Criminal Justice,* 602.

Eggins, E., Mazerolle, L., Higginson, A., Hine, L., Walsh, K., Sydes, M., James, Hassal, G., Roetman, S., Wallis, R., and Williams, J. (2021). Criminal justice responses to child sexual abuse material offending: A systematic review and evidence and gap map. *Trends and Issues in Crime and Criminal Justice,* 623.

Eggins, E., Mazerolle, L., Hine, L., McEwan, J., Hassall, G., Roetman, S., and Roetman, S. (2020). Policing child sex offenders and offending: A rapid review of the evaluation literature. Unpublished manuscript. Brisbane, QLD Australia: The University of Queensland.

Engel, R.S., Corsaro, N., Isaza, G.T., and McManus, H.D. (2020). *Examining the Impact of Integrating Communications, Assessment, and Tactics (ICAT) De-escalation Training for the Louisville Metro Police Department: Initial Findings.* https://www.theiacp.org/sites/default/files/Research Center/LMPD_ICAT Evaluation Initial Findings Report_FINAL 09212020.pdf.

Engel, R.S., McManus, H.D., and Herold, T.D. (2020). Does de-escalation training work? A systematic review and call for evidence in police use-of-force reform. *Criminology and Public Policy,* 19(3), 721–759.

Facione, P. (1990). *Critical thinking: A statement of expert consensus for purposes of educational assessment and instruction (The Delphi Report).* https://www.qcc.cuny.edu/socialsciences/ppecorino/CT-Expert-Report.pdf.

Farrell, G. (1995). Preventing repeat victimization. *Crime & Justice,* 19, 469–534.

Farrington, D.P. (1986). Age and crime. *Crime & Justice,* 7, 189–250.

Finn, P. (2011). Critical thinking: Knowledge and skills for evidence-based practice. *Language, Speech, and Hearing Services in Schools,* 42(1), 69–72.

FitzGerald, C., Martin, A., Berner, D., and Hurst, A. (2019). Interventions designed to reduce implicit prejudices and implicit stereotypes in real world contexts: A systematic review. *BMC Psychology.* https://bmcpsychology.biomedcentral.com/articles/10.1186/s40359-019-0299-7.

Flom, H. (2019). Controlling bureaucracies in weak institutional contexts: The politics of police autonomy. *Governance,* 33(3). https://onlinelibrary.wiley.com/doi/10.1111/gove.12445.

Forscher, P.S., Lai, C.K., Axt, J.R., Ebersole, C.R., Herman, M., Devine, P.G., and Nosek, B.A. (2019). A meta-analysis of procedures to change implicit measures. *Journal of Personality and Social Psychology,* 117(3), 522–559.

Gerspacher, N., Al-Rababah, M., Walker, J.B., and Wilson, N.L. (2019). *Community-oriented Policing for CVE Capacity: Adopting the Ethos Through Enhanced Training.* Hedayah.

Getty, R.M., Worrall, J.L., and Morris, R.G. (2016). How far from the tree does the apple fall? Field training officers, their trainees, and allegations of misconduct. *Crime and Delinquency,* 62(6), 821–839.

Goldstein, H. (1979). Improving policing: A problem-oriented approach. *Crime & Delinquency,* 25(2), 236–258.

Goldstein, H. (1990). *Problem-Oriented Policing.* New York: McGraw-Hill.

Goldstein, I.L. (1986). *Training in Organizations: Needs Assessment, Design, and Evaluation.* Monterey, CA: Brooks/Cole.

Goldstein, I.L. (1991). Training in work organizations. In *Handbook of Industrial and Organizational Psychology,* 2 (2nd ed.), 507–619. Palo Alto, CA: Consulting Psychologists Press.

González, Y. (2021). *Authoritarian Police in Democracy: Contested Security in Latin America.* Cambridge University Press.

Gottschalk, P., Holgersson, S., and Karlsen, J. (2009). How knowledge organizations work: The case of detectives. *The Learning Organization,* 16(2), 88–102.

Hagan, J., Schoenfeld, H., and Palloni, A. (2006). The science of human rights, war crimes, and humanitarian emergencies. *Annual Review of Sociology*, 32(1), 329–349. https://doi.org/10.1146/annurev.soc.32.061604.123125.

Harvey, R.J. (1991). Job analysis. In *Handbook of Industrial and Organizational Psychology*, 2, (2nd ed.), 71–163. Palo Alto, CA: Consulting Psychologists Press.

Hassan, M. (2017). The strategic shuffle: Ethnic geography, the internal security apparatus, and elections in Kenya. *American Journal of Political Science*, 61(2), 382–395.

Hayhurst, K.P., Leitner, M., Davies, L., Millar, T., Jones, A., Flentje, R., Hickman, M., Fazel, S., Mayet, S., King, C., Senior, J., Lennox, C., Gold, R., Buck, D., and Shaw, J. (2019). The effectiveness of diversion programmes for offenders using class a drugs: A systematic review and meta-analysis. *Drugs: Education, Prevention and Policy*, 26(2), 113–124.

Herold, T. (2021). *Police Training Methods Needed to Promote the Rule of Law and Protect the Population.* Paper prepared for the Committee on the Evidence to Advance Reform in the Global Security and Justice Sectors, National Academies of Sciences, Engineering, and Medicine. https://www.nationalacademies.org/event/05-27-2021/evidence-to-advance-reform-in-the-global-security-and-justice-sectors-workshop-2-public-session-1.

Hindelang, M., Hirschi, T., and Weis, J. (1981). *Measuring Delinquency.* Sage.

Hinton, M.S. (2006). *The State on the Streets: Police and Politics in Argentina and Brazil.* Lynne Rienner Publishers.

Holland, A.C. (2015). The distributive politics of enforcement. *American Journal of Political Science*, 59(2), 357–371.

Hundersmarck, S. (2009). Police recruit training: Facilitating learning between the academy and field training. *FBI Law Enforcement Bulletin*, 78(8), 26–31.

Institute of Medicine. (2010). *Redesigning Continuing Education in the Health Professions.* Washington, DC: The National Academies Press. https://doi.org/10.17226/12704.

Jamieson, J.P., Mendes, W.B., Blackstock, E., and Schmader, T. (2010). Turning the knots in your stomach into bows: Reappraising arousal improves performance on the GRE. *Journal of Experimental Social Psychology*, 46(1), 208–212.

Kahn, K.B., and Martin, K.D. (2020). The social psychology of racially biased policing: Evidence-based policy responses. *Policy Insights from the Behavioral and Brain Sciences*, 7(2), 107–114.

Kahneman, D. (2003). A perspective on judgment and choice: Mapping bounded rationality. *American Psychologist*, 58, 697–720.

Kahneman, D. (2011). *Thinking, Fast and Slow.* New York: Macmillan.

Kane, E., Evans, E., and Shokraneh, F. (2018). Effectiveness of current policing-related mental health interventions: A systematic review. *Criminal Behaviour and Mental Health*, 28(2), 108–119.

Kennedy, D.M. (1997). Pulling levers: Chronic offenders, high-crime settings, and a theory of prevention. *Valparaiso University Law Review*, 31(2), 449–484.

Kochel, T.R., and Weisburd, D. (2019). The impact of hot spots policing on collective efficacy: Findings from a randomized field trial. *Justice Quarterly*, 36(5), 900–928.

Koerner, S., Staller, M.S., and Kecke, A. (2020). "There must be an ideal solution…" Assessing training methods of knife defense performance of police recruits. *Policing*, 44(3), 483–497.

Koper, C.S. (1995). Just enough police presence: Reducing crime and disorderly behavior by optimizing patrol time in crime hot spots. *Justice Quarterly*, 12(4), 649–672.

Koper, C.S., Lum, C., Wu, X., and Hegarty, T. (2021). The long-term and system-level impacts of institutionalizing hot spot policing in a small city. *Policing: A Journal of Policy and Practice*, 15(2), 1110–1128.

Koper, C.S., Wu, X., and Lum, C. (2021). Calibrating police activity across hot spot and non-hot spot areas. *Police Quarterly*, 24(3), 382–406. https://doi.org/10.1177/1098611121995809.

La Vigne, N., Jannetta, J., Fontaine, J., Lawrence, D. S., and Esthappan, S. (2019). *The National Initiative for Building Community Trust and Justice: Key Process and Outcome Evaluation Findings*. https://www.urban.org/sites/default/files/publication/100704/national_initiative_for_building_community_trust_and_justice_3.pdf.

Lee, Y., Eck, J.E., O, S-H., and Martinez, N.N. (2017). How concentrated is crime at places? A systematic review from 1970 to 2015. *Crime Science, 6*(1), 1–16.

Livingston, J.D. (2016). Contact between police and people with mental disorders: A review of rates. *Psychiatric Services, 67*(8), 850–857.

Lonsway, K.A. (1996). Police training in sexual assault response: Comparison of approaches. Dissertation. University of Illinois at Urbana-Champaign.

Lum, C., and Koper, C.S. (2017). *Evidence-Based Policing: Translating Research into Practice*. New York: Oxford University Press.

Lum, C., and Nagin, D.S. (2017). Reinventing American policing. *Crime and Justice, 46*, 339–393.

Lum, C., Telep C., Koper, C., and Grieco, J. (2012). Receptivity to Research in Policing. *Justice Research and Policy, 14*(1), 61–95. https://doi.org/10.3818/JRP.14.1.2012.61.

MacQueen, S., and Bradford, B. (2017). Where did it all go wrong? Implementation failure—and more—in a field experiment of procedural justice policing. *Journal of Experimental Criminology, 13*(3), 321–345.

Martin, R.H. (2020). A framework of U.S. contemporary police training: Select types of basic training and purpose of field, inservice, and specialized training. *Journal of Education and Training Studies, 8*(7), 1.

Martinez, N.N., Lee, Y., Eck, J.E., and SooHyun, O. (2017). Ravenous wolves revisited: A systematic review of offending concentration. *Crime Science, 6*(1), 1–16.

Mattarella-Micke, A., Mateo, J., Kozak, M.N., Foster, K., and Beilock, S.L. (2011). Choke or thrive? The relation between salivary cortisol and math performance depends on individual differences in working memory and math anxiety. *Emotion, 11*(4), 1000–1005.

Mazerolle, L. (2021). Core knowledge and skills needed for police to promote the rule of law and protect the population. Paper prepared for the Committee on the Evidence to Advance Reform in the Global Security and Justice Sectors, National Academies of Sciences, Engineering, and Medicine. https://www.nationalacademies.org/event/05-27-2021/evidence-to-advance-reform-in-the-global-security-and-justice-sectors-workshop-2-public-session-1.

Mazerolle, L., and Ransley, J. (2006). *Third Party Policing*. Cambridge University Press.

Mazerolle, L., Bennett, S., Antrobus, E., Cardwell, S.M., Eggins, E., and Piquero, A.R. (2019). Disrupting the pathway from truancy to delinquency: A randomized field trial test of the longitudinal impact of a school engagement program. *Journal of Quantitative Criminology, 35*(4), 663–689.

Mazerolle, L., Bennett, S., Antrobus, E., and Eggins, E. (2012). Procedural justice, routine encounters and citizen perceptions of police: Main findings from the Queensland Community Engagement Trial (QCET). *Journal of Experimental Criminology, 8*(4), 343–367.

Mazerolle, L., Cherney, A., Eggins, E., Higginson, A., Hine, L., and Belton, E. (2021). Multi-agency programmes with police as a partner for reducing radicalisation to violence. *Campbell Systematic Reviews, 17*(2).

Mazerolle, L., Eggins, E., Bennett, S., Roetman, S., Hine, L., McEwan, J., Hassall, G., and Hockey, A. (2019). *Road Policing and Level of Centralisation. A Rapid Review of the Evaluation Literature: Final Report*. The University of Queensland.

McCraty, R., and Atkinson, M. (2012). Resilience training program reduces physiological and psychological stress in police officers. *Global Advances in Health and Medicine, 1*(5), 44–66.

McGinley, B., Agnew-Pauley, W., Tompson, L., and Belur, J. (2019). Police recruit training programmes: A systematic map of research literature. *Policing, 14*(1), 52–75.

McLean, K., Wolfe, S.E., Rojek, J., Alpert, G.P., and Smith, M.R. (2020). Randomized controlled trial of social interaction police training. *Criminology and Public Policy, 19*(3), 805–832.

Moffitt, T.E. (2015). Life-course-persistent versus adolescence-limited antisocial behaviour. In D. Cicchetti and D.J. Cohen (Eds.), *Developmental Psychopathology: Risk, Disorder, and Adaptation,* 570–589. New York: John Wiley & Sons.

Moore, D.E., J.S. Green, and H.A. Gallis. (2009). Achieving desired results and improved outcomes: Integrating planning and assessment throughout learning activities. *Journal of Continuing Education in the Health Professions, 29*(1), 1–15.

Morgan, J. (2021). Policing under disability law. *Stanford Law Review, 73*(6).

Mugford, R., Corey, S., and Bennell, C. (2013). Improving police training from a cognitive load perspective. *Policing, 36*(2), 312–337.

Murphy, K., Mazerolle, L., and Bennett, S. (2014). Promoting trust in police: Findings from a randomised experimental field trial of procedural justice policing. *Policing and Society, 24*(4), 405–424.

Nagin, D.S., Solow, R.M., and Lum, C. (2015). Deterrence, criminal opportunities, and police. *Criminology, 53*(1), 74–100.

National Academies of Sciences, Engineering, and Medicine (NASEM). (2018a). *How People Learn II: Learners, Contexts, and Cultures.* Washington, DC: The National Academies Press. https://doi.org/10.17226/24783.

National Academies of Sciences, Engineering, and Medicine. (NASEM). (2018b). *Learning Through Citizen Science: Enhancing Opportunities by Design.* Washington, DC: The National Academies Press. https://doi.org/10.17226/25183.

National Academies of Sciences, Engineering, and Medicine (NASEM). (2018c). *Proactive Policing: Effects on Crime and Communities.* Washington, DC: The National Academies Press.

National Academies of Sciences, Engineering, and Medicine (NASEM). (2020). *Promoting Positive Adolescent Health Behaviors and Outcomes: Thriving in the 21st Century.* Washington, DC: The National Academies Press. https://doi.org/10.17226/25552.

National Academies of Sciences, Engineering, and Medicine (NASEM). (2021). *Policing to Promote the Rule of Law and Protect the Population: An Evidence-based Approach.* Washington, DC: The National Academies Press.

National Research Council (NRC). (2004). *Fairness and Effectiveness in Policing: The Evidence.* Washington, DC: The National Academies Press.

National Research Council (NRC). (2013). *Improving Self-Escape from Underground Coal Mines.* Washington, DC: The National Academies Press. https://doi.org/10.17226/18300.

Neyroud, F. (2018). *A Narrative Review of Suicidal Ideation as a Predictor of Domestic Homicide, Mass Shootings and Suicide Terrorism.* William Harvey Research Institute, Barts and the London School of Medicine and Dentistry.

Neyroud, P. (2021). Policing "landscapes" for the rule of law and public protection: A review of the available evidence on organizational policies, structures, and human resources. Paper prepared for the Committee on the Evidence to Advance Reform in the Global Security and Justice Sectors, National Academies of Sciences, Engineering, and Medicine. https://www.nationalacademies.org/event/03-24-2021/evidence-to-advance-reform-in-the-global-security-and-justice-sectors-workshop-1-public-session-1.

Noe, R.A. (2010). *Employee Training and Development* (5th ed.). New York: McGraw-Hill Irwin.

O, S., Martinez, N.N., Lee, Y., and Eck, J.E. (2017). How concentrated is crime among victims? A systematic review from 1977 to 2014. *Crime Science*, 6(1), 9. https://doi.org/10.1186/s40163-017-0071-3.

O'Donnell, G. (2004). The quality of democracy: Why the rule of law matters. *Journal of Democracy*, 15(4), 32–46.

Ottoson, J.M., and Patterson, I. (2000). Contextual influences on learning application in practice: An extended role for process evaluation. *Evaluation & the Health Professions*, 23(2), 194–211.

Ouellet, M., Hashimi, S., Gravel, J., and Papachristos, A.V. (2019). Network exposure and excessive use of force: Investigating the social transmission of police misconduct. *Criminology and Public Policy*, 18(3), 675–704.

Owens, E., Weisburd, D., Amendola, K.L., and Alpert, G.P. (2018). Can you build a better cop? Experimental evidence on supervision, training, and policing in the community. *Criminology and Public Policy*, 17(1), 41–87.

Payne, J., Kwiatkowski, M., and Wundersitz, J. (2008). *Police Drug Diversion: A Study of Criminal Offending Outcomes*. Canberra: Australian Institute of Criminology.

Petrosino, A., Turpin-Petrosino, C., and Guckenburg, S. (2010). Formal system processing of juveniles: Effects on delinquency. *Campbell Systematic Reviews*, 6(1), 1–88.

Platz, D., Sargeant, E., and Strang, H. (2017). Effects of recruit training on police attitudes towards diversity: A randomised controlled trial of a values education programme. *Cambridge Journal of Evidence-Based Policing*, 1(4), 263–279.

Police Executive Research Forum. (2018). *The Police Response to Mass Demonstrations: Promising Practices and Lessons Learned*. Washington, DC: Office of Community Oriented Policing Services.

Powell, M.B. (2013). An overview of current initiatives to improve child witness interviews about sexual abuse. *Current Issues in Criminal Justice*, 25(2), 711–720.

Profetto-McGrath, J. (1999). *Critical Thinking Skills and Critical Thinking Dispositions of Baccalaureate Nursing Students*. https://era.library.ualberta.ca/items/fd408428-4eb8-41dc-9ab0-87ae2fcc321e/view/79c80043-f6bb-4171-b0cd-46890880e6cd/NQ39582.pdf.

Profetto-McGrath, J. (2005). Critical thinking and evidence-based practice. *Journal of Professional Nursing*, 21(6), 364–371.

Rajah, V.K. (2012). Panel discussion: Measuring the rule of law. *Singapore Journal of Legal Studies*, 331–356. http://www.jstor.org/stable/24872215.

Ratcliffe, J.H. (2002). Aoristic signatures and the spatio-temporal analysis of high-volume crime patterns. *Journal of Quantitative Criminology*, 18(1), 23–43.

Ratcliffe, J.H. (2015). Towards an index for harm-focused policing. *Policing (Oxford)*, 9(2), 164–182.

Ratcliffe, J.H. (2016). Central American police perception of street gang characteristics. *Policing and Society*, 26(3), 291–311. https://doi.org/10.1080/10439463.2014.942849.

Ratcliffe, J.H., Strang, S.J., and Taylor, R.B. (2014). Assessing the success factors of organized crime groups: Intelligence challenges for strategic thinking. *Policing: An International Journal*, 37(1), 206–227. https://doi.org/10.1108/PIJPSM-03-2012-0095.

Rawson, K.A., and Dunlosky, J. (2011). Optimizing schedules of retrieval practice for durable and efficient learning: How much is enough? *Journal of Experimental Psychology: General*, 140(3), 283–302.

Reaves, B.A. (2016). *State and Local Law Enforcement Training Academies, 2013*. NCJ 249784. Washington, DC: Bureau of Justice Statistics, U.S. Department of Justice. https://bjs.ojp.gov/content/pub/pdf/slleta13.pdf.

Robinson, A.L. (2006). Reducing repeat victimization among high-risk victims of domestic violence: The benefits of a coordinated community response in Cardiff, Wales. *Violence Against Women*, 12(8), 761–788.

Roehl, J., O'Sullivan, C., and Webster, D. (2005). *Assessing Risks from Violent Intimate Partners*. https://www.ojp.gov/ncjrs/virtual-library/abstracts/intimate-partner-violence-risk-assessment-validation-study-rave.

Rosenbaum, D.P., and Lawrence, D.S. (2017). Teaching procedural justice and communication skills during police–community encounters: Results of a randomized control trial with police recruits. *Journal of Experimental Criminology, 13*(3), 293–319.

Rosenfeld, R., Deckard, M.J., and Blackburn, E. (2014). The effects of directed patrol and self-initiated enforcement on firearm violence: A randomized controlled study of hot spot policing. *Criminology, 52*(3), 428–449.

Rouiller, J.Z., and Goldstein, I.L. (1993). The relationship between organizational transfer climate and positive transfer of training. *Human Resource Development Quarterly, 4*(4), 377–390. doi.org/10.1002/hrdq.3920040408.

Sabet, D. (2012). *Police Reform in Mexico: Informal Politics and the Challenge of Institutional Change*. Stanford University Press.

Sahin, N., Braga, A.A., Apel, R., and Brunson, R.K. (2017). The impact of procedurally-just policing on citizen perceptions of police during traffic stops: The Adana randomized controlled trial. *Journal of Quantitative Criminology, 33*(4), 701–726.

Salas, E., Tannenbaum, S.I., Kraiger, K., and Smith-Jentsch, K.A. (2012). The science of training and development in organizations: What matters in practice. *Psychological Science in the Public Interest, 13*(2), 74–101.

Sampson, R.J., Raudenbush, S.W., and Earls, F. (1997). Neighborhoods and violent crime: A multilevel study of collective efficacy. *Science, 277*(5328), 918–924.

Schalkoff, C.A., Lancaster, K.E., Gaynes, B.N., Wang, V., Pence, B.W., Miller, W.C., and Go, V.F. (2020). The opioid and related drug epidemics in rural Appalachia: A systematic review of populations affected, risk factors, and infectious diseases. *Substance Abuse, 41*(1), 35–69.

Schmidt, R.A., and Bjork, R.A. (1992). New conceptualizations of practice: Common principles in three paradigms suggest new concepts for training. *Psychological Science, 3*(4), 207–217.

Sherman, L.W. (1978). *Scandal and Reform: Controlling Police Corruption*. Berkeley: University of California Press.

Sherman, L.W. (1990). Police crackdowns: Initial and residual deterrence. *Crime and Justice, 12*, 1–48.

Sherman, L.W. (1998). *Evidence-Based Policing*. Ideas in American Policing Series. Washington, DC: Police Foundation. https://www.policefoundation.org/wp-content/uploads/2015/06/Sherman-1998-Evidence-Based-Policing.pdf.

Sherman, L.W. (2007). The power few: Experimental criminology and the reduction of harm. *Journal of Experimental Criminology, 3*(4), 299–321.

Sherman, L.W. (2013). The rise of evidence-based policing: Targeting, testing, and tracking. *Crime and Justice, 42*(1), 377–451.

Sherman, L.W., and Harris, H.M. (2015). Increased death rates of domestic violence victims from arresting vs. warning suspects in the Milwaukee Domestic Violence Experiment (MilDVE). *Journal of Experimental Criminology, 11*(1), 1–20.

Sherman, L., and Smith, D. (1992). Crime, punishment and stake in conformity: Legal and extralegal control of domestic violence. *American Sociological Review, 57*(5), 680–690.

Sherman, L.W., Gartin, P., and Buerger, M. (1989). Hot spots of predatory crime: Routine activities and the criminology of place. *Criminology, 27*(1), 27–56.

Sherman, L., Gottfredson, D., MacKensie, D., Eck, J., Reuter, P., and Bushway, S. (1998). *Preventing Crime: What Works, What Doesn't, What's Promising*. National Institute of Justice Research in Brief. https://www.ojp.gov/pdffiles/171676.pdf.

Sloman, S.A. (1996). The empirical case for two systems of reasoning. *Psychological Bulletin, 119*(1), 3–22.

Soderstrom, N.C., and Bjork, R.A. (2015). Learning versus performance: An integrative review. *Perspectives on Psychological Science, 10*(2), 176–199.

Sparrow, M.K. (2008). *The Character of Harms: Operational Challenges in Control.* Cambridge University Press.

Spencer, K.B., Charbonneau, A.K., and Glaser, J. (2016). Implicit bias and policing. *Social and Personality Psychology Compass, 10*(1), 50–63.

Staib, S. (2003). Teaching and measuring critical thinking. *Journal of Nursing Education, 42*(11), 498–508.

Stanovich, K.E., and West, R.F. (2000). Individual differences in reasoning: Implications for the rationality debate? *Behavioral and Brain Sciences, 23*(5), 645–665.

Tankebe, J. (2020). Unintended negative outcomes of counter-terrorism policing: Procedural (in)justice and perceived risk of recruitment into terrorism. *Understanding Recruitment to Organized Crime and Terrorism.* Cham: Springer.

Taylor, B.D. (2014). Police reform in Russia: The policy process in a hybrid regime. *Post-Soviet Affairs, 30*(2-3), 226–255.

Telep, C.W. (2016a). Expanding the scope of evidence-based policing. *Criminology and Public Policy, 15*(1), 243–252.

Telep, C.W. (2016b). Police officer receptivity to research and evidence-based policing: Examining variability within and across agencies. *Crime & Delinquency.* https://journals.sagepub.com/doi/full/10.1177/0011128716642253.

Telep, C.W., and Lum, C. (2014). The receptivity of officers to empirical research and evidence-based policing: An examination of survey data from three agencies. *Police Quarterly, 17*(4), 359–385. https://doi.org/10.1177/1098611114548099.

Telep, C.W., Lum, C., Koper, C.S., and Grieco, J. (2012). Receptivity to research in policing. *Justice Research and Policy, 14*, 61–95.

Townsley, M., Homel, R., and Chaseling, J. (2000). Repeat burglary victimisation: Spatial and temporal patterns. *Australian & New Zealand Journal of Criminology, 33*(1), 37–63.

Turner, E., Medina, J., and Brown, G. (2019). Dashing hopes? The predictive accuracy of domestic abuse risk assessment by police. *British Journal of Criminology, 59*(5), 1013–1034.

Ungar, M. (2002). *Elusive Reform: Democracy and the Rule of Law in Latin America.* Lynne Rienner Publishers.

U.S. Department of State. (2016). *INL Guide to Police Assistance.* Washington, DC: U.S. Department of State, Bureau of International Narcotics and Law Enforcement Affairs. https://2009-2017.state.gov/documents/organization/263419.pdf.

Vander Kooi, G.P., and Palmer, L.B. (2014). Problem-based learning for police academy students: Comparison of those receiving such instruction with those in traditional programs. *Journal of Criminal Justice Education, 25*(2), 175–195.

Versteeg, M., and Ginsburg, T. (2017). Measuring the rule of law: A comparison of indicators. *Law & Social Inquiry, 42*(1), 100–137. https://doi.org/10.1111/lsi.12175.

Vodde, R.F. (2009). *Andragogical Instruction for Effective Police Training.* New York: Cambria Press.

Vodde, R.F. (2012). Changing paradigms in police training: Transitioning from a traditional to an andragogical model. *Police Organization and Training: Innovations in Research and Practice,* 27–44. Springer.

Wang, J., Rao, H., Wetmore, G.S., Furlan, P.M., Korczykowski, M., Dinges, D.F., and Detre, J.A. (2005). Perfusion functional MRI reveals cerebral blood flow pattern under psychological stress. *Proceedings of the National Academy of Sciences of the United States of America, 102*(49), 17804–17809.

Weinborn, C., Ariel, B., Sherman, L.W., and O'Dwyer, E. (2017). Hotspots vs. harmspots: Shifting the focus from counts to harm in the criminology of place. *Applied Geography, 86,* 226–244.

Weisburd, D.L., Telep, C.W., Hinkle, J.C., and Eck, J.E. (2010). Is problem-oriented policing effective in reducing crime and disorder? Findings from a Campbell systematic review. *Criminology & Public Policy, 9*(1), 139–172.

Weisburd, D. (2015). The law of crime concentration and the criminology of place. *Criminology, 53*(2), 133–157.

Weisburd, D., White, C., and Wooditch, A. (2020). Does collective efficacy matter at the micro geographic level? Findings from a study of street segments. *The British Journal of Criminology, 60*(4), 873–891.

Werth, E.P. (2011). Scenario training in police academies: Developing students' higher-level thinking skills. *Police Practice and Research, 12*(4), 325–340.

West, D.J., and Farrington, D.P. (1977). *The Delinquent Way of Life.* London: Heinemann.

Westera, N.J., Powell, M.B., Milne, B., and Goodman-Delahunty, J. (2019). Police interviewing of sexual assault victims: Current organizational responses and recommendations for improvement. *Handbook of Legal and Investigative Psychology,* 182–196. Routledge.

Wheller, L., and Morris, J. (2010). *Evidence Reviews: What Works in Training, Behaviour Change and Implementing Guidance?* UK: National Policing Improvement Agency. https://whatworks.college.police.uk/Research/Documents/What_Works_in_Training_and_Behaviour_change_REA.pdf.

Wheller, L., Quinton, P., Fildes, A., and Mills, A. (2013). *The Greater Manchester Police Procedural Justice Training Experiment.* Coventry, UK: College of Policing. https://whatworks.college.police.uk/Research/Documents/GMP_Technical_Report_Final.pdf.

Williams, S., and Coupe, T. (2017). Frequency vs. length of hot spots patrols: A randomised controlled trial. *Cambridge Journal of Evidence-Based Policing, 1*(1), 5–21.

Wilson, D.B., Brennan, I., and Olaghere, A. (2018). Police-initiated diversion for youth to prevent future delinquent behaviour: A systematic review. *Campbell Systematic Reviews, 14*(1), 1–88.

Wolfgang, M.E., Figlio, R.M., and Sellin, T. (1972). *Delinquency in a Birth Cohort.* University of Chicago Press.

Worden, R.E., Mclean, S.J., Engel, R.S., Cochran, H., Corsaro, N., Reynolds, D., Najdowski, C.J., and Isaza, G.T. (2020). *The Impacts of Implicit Bias Awareness Training in the NYPD.* https://www1.nyc.gov/assets/nypd/downloads/pdf/analysis_and_planning/impacts-of-implicit-bias-awareness-training-in- the-nypd.pdf.

Wright, A. (2018). *Police Interactions with Individuals with Developmental Disabilities: Use of Force, Training, and Implicit Bias.* Stanford Law School. https://law.stanford.edu/wp-content/uploads/2018/11/Alyssa-Wright-Police-Interactions-with-Individuals-with-Developmental-Disabilities-1.pdf.

Xie, M., and Lynch J.P. (2017). The effects of arrest, reporting to the police, and victim services on intimate partner violence. *Journal of Research in Crime and Delinquency, 54*(3), 338–378.

Appendix

Biographical Sketches of Committee Members and Staff

Lawrence W. Sherman (*Chair*) is the Wolfson professor of criminology (emeritus) and director of the Police Executive Programme at the University of Cambridge Institute of Criminology. He previously served as head of the criminology departments at Cambridge, University of Pennsylvania, and University of Maryland, and as president of the American Society of Criminology, the American Academy of Political and Social Science, and the Academy of Experimental Criminology. He has designed or led over 50 randomized field experiments in police agencies on three continents, which formed the basis for his leadership of the global professional movement for evidence-based policing, notably through the U.K. Society for Evidence-Based Policing and its counterparts in Australia, Canada, New Zealand, and the United States. He has advised governments on police policy and trained senior police leaders in multiple countries. As one of six authors of the report to the U.S. Congress *Preventing Crime: What Works, What Doesn't, What's Promising,* he wrote the chapter Maryland Scientific Methods Scale for rank-ordering the strength of evidence from impact evaluations, which has been adapted by a number of governments for their "what works" agendas on crime prevention. He has edited two volumes of the *ANNALS of the American Academy of Political and Social Science* on police and violence, most recently on reducing fatal police shootings. Sherman earned his Ph.D. in sociology from Yale University.

Beatriz Abizanda is a senior specialist in the citizen security cluster of the Inter-American Development Bank (IDB). Her professional experience spans the private and public sectors in Latin America and Europe. She has led the design, implementation, and technical advisory of major IDB criminal justice reform projects in the citizen security sector. Her projects include police modernization, prison reform, and youth violence prevention components for programs in Belize, Brazil, Colombia, Costa Rica, Ecuador, and Uruguay. She has also co-authored the IDB's conceptual framework and operational guidelines for citizen security and coexistence and contributed to the World Bank's World Development Report. She is currently conducting meta-analytic research on the effectiveness of interventions for domestic violence perpetrators. She is a member of the jury of the Stockholm Prize in criminology and is on the editorial board of the *Journal of International Criminology*. Abizanda received a M.A. in criminology from the University of Cambridge and an MBA from Georgetown University.

Abigail Allen is an associate program officer with the National Academies of Sciences, Engineering, and Medicine's Committee on Law and Justice. Her research and writing have been centered on projects related to COVID-19's impact on the factory farming industry and aquatic animal law issues. Allen received her B.A. in criminology, law, and society and a J.D. from George Mason University.

Emily Backes is associate director of the Committee on Law and Justice in the Division of Behavioral and Social Sciences and Education at the National Academies of Sciences, Engineering, and Medicine. She has served as the study director for the reports *The Promise of Adolescence: Realizing Opportunity for All Youth* and *Transforming the Financing of Early Care and Education*. She is currently the study director for the Committee on the Assessment of Health Outcomes by Birth Settings. In her time at the National Academies, she has directed studies and provided analytical and editorial assistance to projects covering a range of topics, including juvenile justice, policing, forensic science, illicit markets, science literacy, science communication, and human rights. Backes received an M.A. and B.A. in history from the University of Missouri, specializing in U.S. human rights policy and international law. She also received a J.D. from the University of the District of Columbia, where she represented clients as a student attorney with the Low-income Taxpayer Clinic and the Juvenile and Special Education Law Clinic.

Yanilda María González is an assistant professor of public policy at the Harvard Kennedy School. Her research focuses on policing, state violence, and citizenship in democracy, examining how race, class, and other forms of inequality shape these processes. Her book *Authoritarian Police in Democracy: Contested Security in Latin America* studies the persistence of police forces as authoritarian enclaves in otherwise democratic states, demonstrating how ordinary democratic politics in unequal societies can both reproduce authoritarian policing and bring about rare moments of expansive reforms. Previously, she was an assistant professor at the School of Social Service Administration at the University of Chicago and has worked at a number of human rights organizations in the United States and Argentina, including the New York Civil Liberties Union, and Equipo Latino Américano de Justicia y Género. González received her Ph.D. in politics and social policy from Princeton University.

Guy Grossman is professor of political science at the University of Pennsylvania. His research is in applied political economy, with substantive focus on governance, migration, security, and conflict processes. He is founder and co-director of the University of Pennsylvania's Development Research Initiative, a member of the Evidence in Governance and Politics network, faculty affiliate of Stanford's Immigration Policy Lab, and the University of Pennsylvania's Identity & Conflict Lab. He designed and carried out field studies in a large number of developing countries, in collaboration with various international agencies, including the World Bank, the U.K. Department for International Development, the U.S. Agency for International Development, as well as with African governments and local nongovernmental organizations. His work has appeared in *Proceedings of the National Academy of Sciences, the American Political Science Review, American Journal of Political Science, International Organization,* and *The Journal of Politics,* among other journals. Grossman received his M.A. in political philosophy and LL.B. in law from Tel-Aviv University and a Ph.D. in political science from Columbia University.

John L. Hagan is the John D. MacArthur professor of sociology and law at Northwestern University, and his primary areas of expertise are in criminology, criminal justice, and international criminal law. He is a member of the National Academy of Sciences and fellow of the American Academy of Arts and Sciences and the Royal Society of Canada. He is best known with coauthor Alberto Palloni for their mortality estimate of the Darfur genocide published in *Science* and his book coauthored with Wenona Rymond-Richmond *Darfur and the Crime of Genocide*. He is also the author of *Who Are the Criminals? The Politics of Crime Policy from the Age of Roosevelt to the Age of Reagan* and with Bill McCarthy *Mean Streets: Youth Crime and Homelessness*. He has received the John Simon Guggenheim Foundation fellowship, the Stockholm Prize in criminology, the Harry Kalven Prize from the Law & Society Association, and the Cesare Beccaria Gold Medal from the German Society of Criminology. Hagan received his M.A. and Ph.D in sociology from the University of Alberta.

Karen Hall is deputy executive director at the Rule of Law Collaborative. Previously, she was associate professor and director of the master of law program in democratic governance and rule of law at the Ohio Northern University Pettit College of Law. She also served with the U.S. Department of State in its Bureau of International Narcotics and Law Enforcement Affairs. While there, she directed the development and management of assistance to the criminal justice system in Afghanistan as part of the overall U.S. foreign assistance initiative. She has also developed programs dealing with institutional reform, access to justice, protection of women's rights, and legal education. She has lived at the U.S. Embassy in Kabul, Afghanistan, where she directly managed the State Department's criminal justice and corrections programs. In recognition of her work, she earned multiple meritorious and superior honor awards from the State Department. Her teaching interests include international rule of law reform, international law, comparative criminal law, rule of law program design and management, student externship courses and introduction to the American legal system. Her current research involves examining the consequences of the appropriations and administrative processes of the U.S. government in relation to rule of law reform worldwide. Hall received her M.A. in security studies from Georgetown School of Foreign Service and her J.D. from Harvard Law School.

Cynthia Lum is a professor of criminology, law and society, and the director of the Center for Evidence-Based Crime Policy at George Mason University. She is a leading authority on evidence-based policing—an approach to policing reform advocating that research, evaluation, analysis, and scientific processes have "a seat at the table" in law enforcement policymaking and practice. Her research focuses on improving law enforcement patrol and investigative operations through rigorous field research and evaluations. She has also developed numerous tools and strategies to translate and institutionalize research into everyday law enforcement activities. She is the author of *Evidence-Based Policing: Translating Research into Practice,* one of the leading volumes on the subject. She has trained thousands of police officers in the United States and around the world on evidence-based policing strategies and approaches, including for the State Department's International Law Enforcement Academy. Lum received a Ph.D. in criminology and criminal justice from the University of Maryland, College Park.

Emily Owens is a professor of criminology, law, and society as well as economics at the University of California, Irvine. She studies a wide range of topics in the economics of crime, including policing, sentencing, and the impact of local public policies on criminal behavior. Her research examines how government policies affect the prevalence of criminal activity as well as how agents within the criminal justice system, particularly police, prosecutors, and judges, respond to policy changes. She is engaged in ongoing research projects on police training, alcohol regulation, immigration policy, and local economic development programs. Owens received a Ph.D. in economics from the University of Maryland, College Park.

Sarah Perumattam is a senior program assistant with the National Academies of Sciences, Engineering, and Medicine's Committee on Law and Justice and Board on Children, Youth, and Families. Her undergraduate research focused on disaster relief and humanitarian response, culminating in her senior capstone project *Improving HIV/AIDS Treatment in Humanitarian Response: Lessons Learned from Rwanda*. She served as an international teaching assistants' consultant at Brown's Center for Language Studies and studied abroad in Seoul, South Korea, where she worked as a guest editor for the Yonsei University Annals. Perumattam graduated from Brown University with a bachelor's degree in public policy and a specialization in government, law, and ethics.

Julie Anne Schuck (*Study Director*) is a senior program officer at the National Academies of Sciences, Engineering, and Medicine. She has provided analytical, administrative, and editorial support for many studies and workshops and served as a technical writer for many reports. Her projects have covered a wide range of subjects, including law and justice issues; national security; STEM (science, technology, engineering, and mathematic) education; the science of human-system integration; workforce development; and the evaluations of several federal research programs. Notably, she was part of the staff team that supported the committee that produced the report *The Growth of Incarceration in the United States: Exploring Causes and Consequences*. Schuck has a B.S. in engineering physics from the University of California, San Diego, and an M.S. in education from Cornell University.

Justice Tankebe is a lecturer in criminology and a fellow at St. Edmund's College, University of Cambridge. Prior to his current appointment, he was a teaching associate on the Police Executive Programme at the Institute of Criminology, Cambridge. His research interests lie in policing, legitimation and legitimacy, organizational justice, corruption, vigilantism and extra-legal punishment, comparative criminology, sociology of law, crime, and criminal justice in sub-Saharan Africa. Tankebe's current research projects include legitimacy and counter-terrorism policing, corruption among prospective elites, sentencing decision-making in Ghana, the death penalty in Africa, and police self-legitimacy. Tankebe received his Ph.D. in criminology from the University of Cambridge.

Jessalyn Brogan Walker is a program officer with the National Academies of Sciences, Engineering, and Medicine's Committee on Law and Justice. Prior to joining the National Academies, Walker was a programs officer at the Global Center on Cooperative Security. In this position, she worked with international police trainers, officers, and leadership to promote a community-oriented approach to policing throughout their organizations. She led in the development and delivery of curriculum to be incorporated into national-level police academies in Jordan, Kosovo, Nigeria, and Tanzania. She also previously worked at the United States Institute of Peace, where she organized and delivered a host of workshops and trainings on the subject of countering violent extremism with law enforcement, government, and civil society actors. Her research interests include international root causes of crime and violence, global prison and police systems, and identity sensitivity and appreciation. She is coauthor of the book *Community-Oriented Policing for CVE Capacity: Adopting the Ethos through Enhanced Training*. Walker holds an undergraduate degree in sociology and politics and a master's degree in criminology from University College Cork.

Sunia Young is a senior program assistant with the National Academies of Sciences, Engineering, and Medicine's Committee on Law and Justice and Board on Children, Youth, and Families. She previously worked as a case manager at a Washington, DC-based behavioral health organization. Young also interned at the Carter Center's Mental Health Program and with a DC-based organization that supports Asian women who have experienced domestic violence and sexual assault. Additionally, Sunia has studied the Persian language extensively and spent the summer of 2018 in Tajikistan studying the Iranian and Tajik dialects of Persian through the United States Department of State. Young graduated from Davidson College with a bachelor's degree in psychology and a minor in Arab studies.